WALRUS WITH A GOLD TOOTH

CRIME IN ANCHORAGE,
ALASKA—THE PIONEER WAY—UNORGANIZED!

STEVEN C. LEVI

PO Box 221974 Anchorage, Alaska 99522-1974
books@publicationconsultants.com—www.publicationconsultants.com

ISBN 978-1-59433-485-6
eISBN 978-1-59433-486-3
Library of Congress Catalog Card Number: 2014941707

Manufactured in the United States of America.

"To say that the history of Anchorage, Alaska is 'just like every place else,' is like saying that every walrus has a gold tooth."

... Warren Sitka, Alaska humorist

In The Beginning

A t 5:36 p.m., Alaska Standard Time, on March 17, 1964, Good Friday, a tectonic fault near College Fjord in Prince William Sound slipped. Though the earthquake lasted less than three minutes it brought down buildings in Anchorage and created *tsunamis* as high as 220 feet along the Pacific coastline as far south as Crescent City, California. In Kodiak, the ground surged upwards as high as 30 feet. In Valdez, a section of the waterfront 4,000 feet long and 600 feet wide, slipped into Prince William Sound generating a wave 30 feet high that obliterated the rest of the dock area and quite a bit of the city. 30 people died *en masse* in Valdez and further south in Prince William Sound the Native villages of Chenega and Afognak were wiped off the map. Because of its unique geomorphic features, Port Alberni in British Columbia was hit twice by the *tsunami* and 55 homes were washed away. 3,500 miles south of Anchorage, 12 people drowned in the rising waters in Crescent City, California.

In Anchorage, the shaker brought down most of the downtown area. Along Fourth Avenue, from F to C streets, the street level dropped as much as five feet popping support beams and dangerously tilting buildings. The one year-old J. C. Penny's Garage looked as though it were a relic of a bombed-out European city during the Second World War. The sheer concrete walls bulged out and then collapsed. The twisting of the building snapped the load bearing walls and all six floors of the parking structure came pancaking down one upon the other until the structure was nothing more than a steel and cement Dagwood sandwich. One of the 30-odd cars crushed by the collapsing floors gave the disaster a voice: its horn went off and blasted down the deserted streets for three days before the car battery died.

It was the most powerful recorded earthquake up to that time. There were 139 casualties as a result of the disaster. Fifteen died from the earthquake itself and the rest from *tsunamis*.

But what most people did not know was that there was a 140th death, one that did not make it into the history books. The body was found after the quake beneath the collapsed brick wall of the Empress Theatre on Third Avenue in Anchorage. What made the death unusual was that it had two bullet holes in the back of the skull. The demise of the individual, initially identified as Cordova Benson, was reported in the Anchorage Police logbook and the body taken to the makeshift morgue for earthquake victims. Six hours later the body was identified as a manikin and the police officers who initially reported the individual as being Cordova Benson were reassigned other duties.

At that time there was a resident of Anchorage by the name of Cordova Benson, a tavern, brothel and gambling den habitué who lived well with no visible means of support. Those in the know reported him as a front for the New Jersey mob, a rumor the Anchorage Police took as wild speculation considering that the New Jersey mob was in New Jersey and there was a substantial stretch of real estate between the Meadowlands and Cook Inlet. The Anchorage Police Department was certain that Cordova Benson was an alias as both names were streets in Anchorage and the swarthy complexion of the deceased was more Italian or Spanish than Tlingit or Athabaskan. But no one knew for sure and no one could ask Benson as he and two of his associates had disappeared.

To date none of the three have reappeared. The only alleged official reference to the demise of Benson was in the logbook of the Anchorage Police Department for March 28, 1964, a page that, to this day, is missing.

Harold Drochester

" You got that tape recorder running? Yeah, yeah, yeah, I know. It's not a *tape* recorder. They don't make them anymore. Now it's MP3s. I know that. I may be over 90 but I am not some old fogey who got lost in the fog when the digits on the century flipped. Bits and bytes now. Tweets and twerks, jpeg, mpeg tiff, gif, megabyte, kilobyte, Facebook, YouTube, iTunes, eBooks, Kindle, Nook. I know all that. No more reel-to-reel. Let's get started on this.

That's right, I know the ground rules. You gave me a laundry list before you came over, remember? My name is Harold Drochester – not Dorchester, Drochester, D-r-o-c-h-e-s-t-e-r. I know I am on tape and that what I say can and will be used against me in a court of law – *Ha! I'm being funny*! I know I am being recorded and I know what I say will be used against me in the court of history because there isn't time to get me in a real court now. Wasn't the politics to get me then; ain't the time to get me now. I am speaking on the record because a manuscript detailing certain events in the 1950s and 1960s in Anchorage have become public knowledge and I am here to set the record straight. I have been asked by the Alaska Historical Publication Association to make this tape. (Cough)

I am going to give the background and circumstances for the murder of one man, Cordova Benson, which I perpetrated on

March 28 or March 29, 1964, in the day or two days after the Great Alaska Earthquake here in Anchorage. What I will be telling is the truth, the whole truth, nothing but the truth so help me the God I don't believe in. I do this of my own free will and because I no longer give a damn who knows.

Cordova Benson, by the way, was not his real name. 'Course you know that now. The guy's name was actually Al "Big Lip" Marchetti. Maybe. He's still listed as missing out of New Jersey. He called himself Cordova Benson by combining names he heard when he got here. Cordova from the town and Benson from the street for Benny Benson, the Native who designed the Alaska flag.

Before 1964 we didn't have a lot of First Degree murders in Anchorage. Not in those days. Not any money in it. I'm talking First Degree where you hunt someone down like a dog and shoot him dead, where someone plotted to kill someone else. Most of the murders in Anchorage in those days which I do *not* call First Degree but the cops did was for money or women. Today's it's more about drugs. Over time we had a handful of what we used to call "downtown divorces." After about 1970 they were called "Spenard Divorces" where one spouse shoots t'other. That's because the seedy people moved from downtown out to Spenard. They came back to downtown in the 1970s with the oil pipeline boom. When the first boom went away in the 1960s the seedy people went to Spenard. Kind of a boom to bust thing. When there's a boom, my kind of business moves downtown. When the boom is over, we move back to the alleys in Spenard.

Now just for the record, I'm not doing this because I suddenly found God or woke up one morning with Jesus on my mind. I'm not the religious type. Don't go to church. Don't care to go to church. Let's get that out of the way right now. I have an immortal soul and I will talk with the Big Man when I get there. I guess if you didn't know why I did what I did, well, you'd think

I was a bad man. In that, you would be right. I was a bad man. I don't deny it and I don't apologize for it. It was a different time then, a different world. Anchorage ain't what it used to be and will never be that way again. I'm primarily doing this because I'm the last one of that time left. Everyone else has gone on – and then that manuscript suddenly popped up.

As far as my background is concerned, I never really had a normal childhood. Born and raised on a dirt farm in Missouri but we scattered in about 1937, during the Dustbowl. Let me tell you no history book can really describe what happened. It was like the plagues from the Bible. Dust was bad enough but then we had grasshoppers, locusts, and they ate everything. I mean, they even ate the wood handles of the rakes and shovels! Never even knew they could do that. It was a tough winter and the next spring we had a harvest. 'Cept the harvest was rabbits. Millions of them. Coyotes had been starved off the range the winter before so there wasn't anything to eat the rabbits. They were a plague. Hundreds of thousands of them. So many I'd say they came in herds. Nothing to eat them so they just got born and ate everything. Our farm died a slow death. We didn't get hit near as bad as other parts of the Midwest but we got hit good and hard. By 1937 there was no sense in staying. So we scattered. Last time I saw my mam and pap they were on their way to Kansas City. Mom had a sister there. My brother was 18 and he went to Birmingham, why I can't remember. I wasn't going to go to no Kansas City and I sure wasn't going to Birmingham either. So I said my goodbyes and rode the rails to California. I was 16 years old at the time and that was a man in those days.

I wasn't the youngest one on the trains for damn sure. There were a lot of farm boys just like me looking for a meal anywheres. I made it as far as Sacramento. Weather was better but there weren't any jobs. It was the middle of the Depression and I was in and out of soup kitchens and Salvation Army shelters. Drifted across the new Bay Bridge and into San Francisco.

Fantastic city – if you are working. If not, it is wet and cold and miserable. Did not know what I was going to do and one day I thought I had been delivered. Was down on the wharf and this man comes by and says he is hiring. Hiring!

Praises to the gods and saints! He was hiring!

I didn't care what it was, I was interested. Signed on before he finished saying what the job was. I went right out to a ship and spent three days in a cargo hold with a bunch of Mexicans and Japanese and Chinese and whatever and then we headed north to work in the canneries of Alaska. Did not know what I was getting myself into.

But it was a job.

Found myself in Naknek working on a slime line. It was the first regular paycheck that I had ever received. It sure wasn't much but it was something. I also got food and a warm dry place to sleep. I was all of about 18 by then. Spent one season with the Flips, Japs, Greasers and a lot of other folks who didn't speak English at all. That was all I could stand. At the end of the season I had some cash in my pocket and we were going back to San Francisco. I'd been there before I went north and there wasn't a job to be found then and I didn't think it would be any different six months later. But once you are on the boat there ain't much you can do about it.

However, the ship had stopped in Seattle to refuel on the way up so I figured I might be able to jump ship there. I had my pay in my pocket so I didn't have stay onboard all the way back to San Francisco. As it turned out I did not make it as far as Seattle. Something went wrong in the engine room and the ship had to dock in Petersburg. I'd never heard of Petersburg but it was dry land and I saw lots of boats in the harbor. Lots of boats meant lots of people.

Boy, did that turn out to be wrong!

But I didn't know it at the time.

Standing on the rail of that stinking freighter I figured anywhere would be better than San Francisco and this place looked just as good as any to jump ship.

So I did.

I was half-right.

There was a lot of work.

But only during the fishing season.

The rest of the year I was on my own. But that was the first time I made enough money to say I was employed. Considering how I was living, it was good money. I was able to sleep on a warehouse floor during that first winter. It was warm and out of the snow and I traded my bed, so to speak, for acting as a night watchman. There really wasn't anything to watch for. After all, this was Petersburg in 1940. The warehouse owner was an old Norwegian who could barely speak English. Nice guy, heart of gold. He also gave me some good advice: join the Army. I knew there was such a thing as an Army but didn't know much else about it. But he said it paid.

That was good enough for me.

So I joined up and that made a lot of people in Petersburg very happy. It got one homeless person out of town and one local out of the army. There was some kind of a quota and when I went in, someone in Petersburg did not have go. It wasn't that the people in Petersburg were unpatriotic or anything like that. They were fishermen and fish was food. America needed food – even more so when the war started. But there had to be some men from Petersburg going into the military otherwise some government people in town would lose their job.

So I went.

Got to be a Marine. A jarhead. That was fine with me. It was a job. It paid. Could have been the start of a career. Got sent to Parris Island, South Carolina, hot, I tell you, hot like I had never known it. The family farm was in Missouri and it got hot there but not hot like South Carolina. Hell's got to be cooler.

It's that wet heat that melts you. I didn't have to shower, I did it all day long. Like I was in a steam bath— I *was* in a steam bath. Seven weeks in boot and then I was off to San Diego. Spent the winter in the greatest city on earth. I had money like I'd never had before! Not a lot, about $21 a month but room and board were paid. When I wasn't on duty I was on the beach chasing women. Service man heaven.

Until December of the next year.

It was as if God were looking down on me and saying, "Harold, you have yourself a very fine time there in San Diego because I am saving something *very special* for you." Well, He did. I was going to be transferred to the Philippines and was in the barracks in San Francisco when the Nips hit Pearl Harbor. Had they hit Hawaii a week later I would have been in Honolulu. Three weeks later I would have been in Bataan. Might not have made it out of either of those places.

But that's the way my life has always been. Just a week or two one side or the other of a disaster. Guess you could say I have lived a charmed life. Considering I could have been killed on any one of those crappy little islands we invaded I did live a charmed life. A lot of men better than me got it. Yeah, I killed japs, zips, nips. A lot of them. I'm not going to talk about that. I carry those boys with me every day. They were boys, just like me – boys who had no business being there. I didn't have any business being there either. I'm not that kind of a patriot. We were there because that's where our governments wanted us to be. Them and me. That's it. I didn't have a personal quarrel with them or them with me. But there we were and some of us were going to come out alive and everyone else was going to die. I beat the odds. But the ones who did not make it are with me every night, Americans and Japs. The Japs didn't deserve what they got; their Emperor did and he never got his. Son of a bitch died of cancer about 30 years ago. In silk pajamas and the boys he sent to die went down in ditches, sewage ponds and rice paddies. Our son of a bitch died in Warm Spring, Georgia of a stroke. What a way to go. Just poof! Gone.

Now, I'm not here to talk about the war. I'm here to talk about murder. That's what you wanted, right? OK, but it will take some explaining so you have to let me do this my way. Hey, I'm the star here! Yeah, yeah, I'll get to the murder but you gotta have a lot of background first otherwise you won't understand how it went down.

I got out of the Marines the spring after the war ended. 1946. We were all getting out and I sure didn't have a place to go. I wasn't going back to the farm. 'Course I couldn't. I wasn't going back to San Francisco and I sure wasn't going to go back to working on fishing boats in Petersburg. No way was I going back to South Carolina and every place I had been in the Marines was jungle and jungle and more jungle. I had been to Hawaii but it was just jungle then. And pineapple fields. I'd had enough jungle. I didn't have a place to go – but I got a lot of transit money in San Francisco because I had enlisted in Petersburg.

I was wondering about where I was going to go next when I heard that some companies were hiring ex-GIs to work in Alaska. They were doing all kinds of building in the middle of nowhere and they needed men who could take the hard living. That was me. I had been living hard my whole life. Besides, they paid my way north so I could keep my transit money. Better yet, it was cold in Alaska. I'd had my fill of hot weather. Cold would be change.

It also paid better than I had ever made. So I signed up.

Here is where your story begins, h-i-s-t-o-r-i-a-n. Me coming to Anchorage. About 18 months after the war ended. See, back in those days after the Second World War the biggest enemy we had was the Soviet Union, called the USSR in those days, the United Soviets Socialist Republics. Today it's called Russia but it's not the same thing.

If there was any one thing we feared in those days it was the Ruskies. They made Congress wet their collective pants every single night of the year. The Ruskies were big and they were bad and they didn't like us at all. 'Course we didn't like them either. It was a mutual hate and we had to keep watching each other because neither of us trusted the other. Over in Europe they were cutting Europe in half and building a wall in Berlin. On the other side the world there was Alaska and that was why I was Alaska.

Making a very long story very short, we didn't trust the Ruskies so the United States military was expanding big time into Alaska. I mean all the services. While the rest of the country was coming off war footing, Alaska was putting on both boots. There were two massive Air Force bases – remember, there had not been an Air Force before the Second World War. It had been the Army Air Corps. After the war it became the Air Force. That was good news to Alaska because suddenly there were two huge army bases – Fort Richardson in Anchorage and Fort Wainwright in Fairbanks – and now two Air Force bases, Elmendorf in Anchorage and Ladd Field in Fairbanks. Those bases were hopping because they had all kinds of war air craft. In the lower states there are TAC, MAC and SAC bases. TAC is Tactical Air Command and those are the fighter pilots. MAC is Military Air Command and those are the transport people. SAC is Strategic Air Command. SAC had the planes with the nuclear bombs that flew around the USSR waiting to rush in and drop the big ones on the Ruskies – go see DR. STRANGELOVE, funny movie but there's a lot of truth in it.

But Alaska was so large and so close to Russia, or, as we knew it then, the USSR, that we had to have TAC, MAC and SAC planes in Alaska. We had everything up here because we were on the bleeding edge of the Cold War – and you'll have to look that up on your Wikipedia too.

When I signed on for construction in Alaska I was told we were going to be building military bases. Hell that was a snap to me. I'd seen the landing strips get carved out of the jungle by the Seabees and that looked easy. All those boys had to do was sit on bulldozers and road graders and drive into the jungle. Let the machines do the work. Yeah, there were Jap snipers but those boys were making a helluva lot more than I was and I was getting shot at too! I was getting $21 a month; the Seabees were making ten times that much. Construction was the way to go during the war and I figured to get a slice of that pie after the war – and I sure as hell was not going back to San Francisco or Missouri!

But I had no idea how much construction there was going to be in Alaska. I also had no idea what a wild city Anchorage was going to be. It's wasn't just a frontier city. It was a Wild West city in the middle of nowhere. It was 2,000 miles north of Seattle with nothing in-between but a dirt road that was ankle-deep in mud with clouds of mosquitoes the whole way – until it froze solid. The next largest city was Fairbanks, if you could call that a city, and if you wanted to call it *large*. At that time the largest city in Alaska was Juneau at about 5,000. Anchorage and Fairbanks were about 3,400 or 3,500 apiece.

Now it's really important that you understand how fast Anchorage grew. It's important to what you want to know about the murder. Between the Second World War and the Earthquake, from 1944 to 1964, 20 years, Anchorage grew by a factor of **ten**. It was ten times larger in 1964 that it had been in 1944. That was a lot of people and a lot of money. I'll get into the money in a little bit but you have to know what growing by ten times in 20 years means. It was a 20 year boom. Everything just kept growing. Before the war the city only ran to the Park Strip, between 9th and 10th. That was the airport then. That's why there aren't any telephone or power lines across the Park Strip today. When they had to extend telephone service and power onto the other side for the new homes, from 10th Street south, they put the wires underground because the airport was still there.

Don't think of Anchorage as a city in those days; think of it as a war zone. The population was going up so fast that no one could keep up with it. The lounges and bars didn't even have cash registers. No need to. So much money was coming in we just tossed it into a box where the till should have been. Planes were coming in loaded with cement and wood and wire and glass and the barges were double and triple deep at the docks on Ship Creek and more were waiting on Cook Inlet to come in. The sidewalks were like New York, or at least the pictures of New York I have seen. Never been there myself. They were packed, the sidewalks I mean. There weren't that many roads that were paved – the only ones I remember were around the courthouse, now the old courthouse, on Fourth Avenue across from the movie theater. That's why the movie theater was there. Cap Lathrop was no fool. Put his theater on the only paved road in town that had sidewalks.

There was construction in town, downtown, out of town and way out of town. There were buildings erupting from the muskeg. Houses built where I didn't think it was possible to build. Everyone was in the real estate and construction business and a lot of people were making a lot of money. Everyone had money. Lots of it. They were buying everything. I wasn't in the booze and women business yet but I was sure buying booze and women. I was making more in a month smoothing cement than I had in a year of shooting at Japs and I was spending it as fast as I was making it. I could not keep money in my pockets or my trousers buckled!

But that was not even half of the story.

You see – and you, young man, are not old enough to remember the USSR – we were right at the beginning of the Cold War. That was when we, the United States and Europe, were wet in the armpits over the Commies. The Commies in those days were the Red Chinese, Red North Koreans and the Russians. There were two types of Chinese then, China that is now called Taiwan and the mainland country. Mao Tse Tung was the leader of the Chinese people, then called the People's Republic of China and now called China. Chiang Kai-shek was President of China and was being pushed onto that little tiny island. Then there was Korea. Half of it was free courtesy of the Korean War and it was called Korea. The north was being run by a family of stumblebums and it was called the People's Republic of Korea. What we now call Russia was the United Soviets Socialist Republics and it was being run by Stalin who was one *very* nasty fellow. He should have been. The Russians lost 26 million people to the Nazi. But they had 150 million people who survived the war. That made them about as large as we were.

All of this history probably doesn't mean much to you young people but after the Second World War we had real reason to worry about the Commies, particularly in Alaska. It was only a matter of time before Chiang Kai-shek got the boot out of Mainland China. He knew it and so he was shipping money and gold out as fast as planes could carry it. The reason this is important to you – because you are an Alaskan historian – is that one of those planes with about 16 tons of gold went down on Mt. St. Elias. Everyone knows where the plane went down but no one can get the gold because it's in the plane under about 30 feet of ice. The wreckage is in a National Park and that's supposed to keep anyone from picking through the wreckage but, hey, with 16 tons of gold there have been lots of salvage operations.

I'm glad I brought this up. My biggest complaint about historians is that they write everything looking backwards. That is, they have their minds set in *today* and try to write about what it was like *yesterday*. They don't know what it was like! They just make value judgments based on their morals and view point. If something is a bad idea today than it must have been a bad idea then and wonder how come those people in that time didn't understand that it was a bad idea? That's a crock. People were doing the same things then they are doing today. For instance, we were all heavy drinkers in 1950 and we are still heavy drinkers today. The worst drunks then spent all their money on booze and walked home. The worst drunks today get arrested for DUI. Drunks then, drunks now. Nothing has changed.

While we are talking about it, another big difference between what a lot of the Alaskan historians write today and what actually happened is that those historians live uptown. They are working at the university or the library and read the old papers and do not have a clue what it was like to be a working person living downtown. There is a world of difference between what was happening uptown and downtown. Uptown news got written up in the newspaper. What happened downtown was word of mouth. All of us downtown folks knew what was going on. We knew the bad guys and the lawyers, the dipso judges, working girls, pimps, bar tenders and quite a few of the rich men slumming the blind pigs. We all knew each other, knew each other's kinks but we didn't go running to the newspaper. But the damn socialites with the big parties *did* go running to the newspaper. They fought to get into the newspaper. So today you read a lot about what was going on uptown but unless it got real nasty, juicy or strange, downtown news stayed downtown.

What you are going to get from me is the downtown story, the kind of stuff that never made it into the newspapers. I was there from the Second World War until my knees gave out. That's why I'm here in the local old folk's home, God's waiting room for Alaskans. I'm just waiting to check out.

But getting back to Alaska where I left off. At the end of the Second World War America was scared to death of the Commies and there was very good reason for that. The Russians in particular. The Chinese didn't have much then, I mean like nuclear weapons. But the Soviets did. See, they, just like us, had rushed into Berlin and snagged some of the best rocket scientists the world had ever known. Hitler trained 'em and we got 'em. We got a lot of them too. But we didn't get all of them. The Soviets got the ones we didn't.

Both sides had scientists and both sides of the Cold War were building missiles that could carry nuclear bombs. Both sides were building nuclear missiles and bombs lickety-split. It was called the Arms Race then. We were building bigger and nastier missiles and bombs and the Soviets were doing the same thing.

Then the Soviets shut themselves off from the rest of the world. You young people probably remember reading about the Berlin Wall in your history classes but it was more than just a wall. There was a line of electrified fences and moats and minefields from the Baltic Sea to the Mediterranean. There was a wall that divided Berlin in half but Berlin was behind the Iron Curtain and that's the mileage that got the most attention. That was because the Soviets cut off Berlin from the rest of Europe hoping we'd abandon Berlin. But we didn't. We supplied the people of Berlin, our sector in Berlin, with everything they needed with an airlift. It was called the Berlin Airlift and you can read all about it in Wikipedia too.

There is a point to this story, yeah, and it involves Alaska. But you gotta be patient and let me tell it. You're the one who asked for the interview, remember?

We, America, and the European counties who fought with us during the Second World War, formed an alliance called NATO, the North Atlantic Treaty Organization to face off the Soviets in Europe. We had troops on our side of the Iron Curtain and the Soviets had troops on their side of the Iron Curtain. We were building planes and nuclear bombs and missiles on our side and they were doing the same on their side. But that was only in Europe. We were just as concerned about the Red Chinese so we formed another alliance with nations in Southeast Asia called SEATO, the Southeast Asia Treaty Alliance. That was called the Bamboo Curtain and we had our planes and nuclear bombs and missiles on our side and the Chinese had their troops on their side of the Bamboo Curtain. They didn't have nuclear missiles yet but they were going to get them.

Anyway, and I have to finish with NATO before we can go on to Alaska. Every hour of every day we were sweating square nails that the Soviets would launch a sneak attack against Europe. So, to counter the threat we had large planes, bombers, called B-52s. These were known as Stratofortresses. They were long-range, subsonic, jets each carrying two or three nuclear bombs. They would take off in groups and fly along the Iron Curtain and the Bamboo Curtain just in case the commies tried something stupid. These fly boy were at it 24/7. From 1952, where the plane got its name, until the era of Ronald Reagan, we had dozens of B-52s with nuclear bombs on board flying along the borders of the USSR and China. Those groups were part of SAC, the Strategic Air Command. Oh, and the B-52s were called *Buffs* for Big Ugly Folk. I use the term *Folk* because you are going to be giving this tape, MP3, to libraries. So *folk* it is.

Things got nastier when the Soviets started testing nuclear bombs, which told us they had them. Then they started testing missiles, rockets. Then we knew they had those too. The larger ones with more range were called ICBMs, Intercontinental Ballistic Missiles. Which meant that they could be fired from the USSR and hit the American homeland. That meant that a nuclear bomb on an ICBM could be launched from Russia and could hit London, Paris, Sidney, Saigon or Honolulu. As the missiles got better and better, ours and theirs, there was every reason to believe that a missile from the USSR could be fired from, say, Moscow and hit Kansas City or Detroit. It was a scary thought.

Even scarier was the thought that the Soviets might have a very, very big advantage when it came to Alaska. See, and this is where the NATO and SEATO stuff is important, in Europe we had an army to face off the Soviets across the Iron Curtain. In Southeast Asia we had allies to face off the Red Chinese across the Bamboo Curtain. But when it came to Alaska, we didn't have any troops or allies to face off the Soviets across what was called the Ice Curtain. We didn't even have conventional troops in Alaska and Alaska, in some places, is only a few hundred yards from the USSR. We had zip in Alaska after the Second World War. In fact, until the end of the war we were shipping war planes, fighters and bombers, to the Soviet Union out of Alaska.

That's right. War planes were being flown by American crews to Fairbanks and then Soviet crews would take the planes and fly them over the Bering Sea and across Russia to the battlefield. By giving the Russians the planes in Alaska – it started as part of the Lend Lease Program – the planes were thousands of miles closer to the battlefront than flying them across the Atlantic and then through the war zone to Russia over Germany. It was also a lot safer because no one was shooting at them between the assembly factory and Moscow. Flying over Germany every anti-aircraft gun from the Western Front to the Eastern Front would have been taking potshots at those planes.

Like I said, at the end of the Second World War America had pretty close to nothing in Alaska. We had an Ice Curtain, yeah, but we didn't have that many troops on our side. There were some troops on the other side and there were remote bases in Siberia being built but we didn't have anything close in size to what the Soviets had. Worse, as we entered the era of the ICBMs, it wasn't the troop bases in the Soviet Union along the eastern shore of the Bering Sea that were of concern to us. It was the nuclear missile sites in the Russian interior that scared us. The Soviets weren't going to launch the ICBMs from an installation along the shore. They were going to launch the missile from some secret site inside the Soviet Union. We knew they had ICBMs because we had spy satellites looking down. But the problem with a satellite was that it told you what the Soviets had – but nothing was in real time then. In other words, the satellite images were called photographs. They were a snapshot of time. All it told the Pentagon people was what the Soviets had in that $1/2500^{th}$ of a second when the spy satellite snapped its photograph. Even if the satellite had snapped a shot of an ICBM being launched, the Pentagon would not have seen the launch on the images for days and by then it would have been too late to do anything but sweep up the debris of some American city.

Alaska was America's most vulnerable frontier so the Ice Curtain had to be fortified. We had to have troops on our side of the Ice Curtain. But that was the problem. By the time we started pumping troops onto our side, the technology had changed so much that more than troops were necessary. We needed a very sophisticated radar system to track any incoming missiles. See, because of the curvature of the earth, if an ICBM was launched from a secret base in Russia to hit an American target, no one was going to know the missile had been launched – no radar that is – until the missile actually came over the horizon above the curvature of the earth. Once radar picked up the missile we would know it was coming. But the ICBMs were traveling so fast that once a radar base in Alaska picked up an incoming ICBM, the missile would be into the American heartland with an hour or so.

What the Pentagon needed was an early warning alarm system and the only location available to give that early warning was Alaska. And the further out that early warning was, the more time the American heartland would have to prepare. So right after the Second World War, when I went to work construction in Alaska, the military went whole hog making Alaska and Canada the early warning alarm for an ICBM strike. All along the shore of the Arctic Ocean, from the Chukchi Sea to Hudson Bay was a string of Distant Early Warning bases. They were called the DEW line. This was America's – and Canada's – first line of defense. If an ICBM missile was launched from the interior of the Soviet Union, the DEW line radar sites would pick it up as soon as it appears over the curvature of the earth.

But – and this was a very big *but* and is critically important to Alaska history and the story I am telling you – the DEW line had been built in the 1940s and at that time off-the-wire communication meant radio and radio was not all that good. It was critical for these DEW line sites to be able to communicate with the Pentagon clearly and in real time. The communication also had to be secure. So the United States military built what was then a state-of-the-art communication system. It was called White Alice and, no, I do not know why it was called White Alice. It was just called White Alice. The White Alice bases, and there were about 30 of them in Alaska, were these big, hulking buildings with massive antennas that were four or five stories tall. The communication system was microwave and it was line-of-sight. This meant that the stations had to be built in exactly the right spot so that the signal from the DEW line would go straight – and I mean straight – down a line of White Alice sites. The signal would be boosted in power at each station and then sent along to the next one. The final stop would be in Fairbanks or Anchorage and then the message would passed along to the Pentagon or wherever by a regular phone line.

This was all fine and good but the military – and you know how the military thinks – you cannot have just a Plan A. You have to have a Plan B. Plan B was that the Soviets would probably make a preliminary strike with a missile and follow it up with an invasion. That invasion in Alaska would have to come by air. So we had to be prepared for that invasion. We knew it was going to coming in by air, in planes, so we had to be prepared for the armada of Soviet aircraft coming in and the tens of thousands of men that were going to get off those planes. The key to the success of Alaska was to stop the Soviet planes before they ever landed and disgorged all those Russian soldiers. That was the plan.

So we had to bolster our defenses. The way we did that was by building a string of AC&WS, Aircraft Warning System, bases. These were radar bases that were meant to watch for incoming Soviet planes. Remember, the DEW line was tracking in-coming ICBMs but the AC&WS bases were built to track in-coming aircraft. Once any Russian aircraft was picked up on radar, the Air Force would scramble fighters out of Elmendorf and Ladd Field. With luck, the fighters would knock the Russians out of the sky well before any planes got to Anchorage or Fairbanks. Those AC&WS sites were part of NORAD, the North American Air Defense. I know there are a lot of acronyms here but they are all important. Now let me continue.

Then there were the United States Coast Guard LORAN stations, Long Range Aid to Navigation. There weren't any good maps in those days and most of the pilots up here were not from Alaska. They didn't know Mt. McKinley from an elephant's butt. No one had GPS in those days so they used LORAN. Ask any old pilot what LORAN is. He'll remember the bad old days. I guess there were 20 LORAN bases in Alaska and a Navy base in Unalaska and a load of Search and Rescue boats at sea.

On top of that we had the secret agent program! See, the CIA figured – yeah, that CIA, our CIA – figured that the Russians, Soviets might invade so they got a bunch of Alaskans to be part of a stay-behind program. These were people, James Bond kinds, who were supposed to stay in place when the Soviets invaded. The CIA gave them radios and medicine and stuff like that and had them hide all that equipment out in the wilderness. Can you imagine that?

From the look on your face you think this is a bunch of old fogey crap, that it doesn't have anything to do with the murder you want to know about. Well you young people have to learn that there is no such thing as the present. The *present* is just the razor's edge where the past meets the future. Every problem we have now came from the past. We have the problem because someone in the past didn't solve the problem then. Now it's your problem. Want to do your kids and grandkids a favor? Solve the problems of today today. Let them solve the problems of tomorrow without getting sucked into the problems you should have solved today, problems like drunk drivers, drug abuse, care for the mentally incompetent, gun control, the right to die. These are all going to be hot button issues when I'm gone because my generation didn't have the brains or *cojones* to solve them in our generation.

Now back to the past. This military buildup during the Cold War is what made the economy of the world. Ever hear of the "military-industrial complex?" No? Well, you are going to be hearing a lot about it in your generation because we could not solve that problem in ours. All this talk about SAC, TAC, MAC, DEW line and AC&WS may seem like ancient history of you but the United States spent billions of dollars on those sites. We had SAC bombers on military bases and all over the world. There were AC&WS sites all over the world. There were LORAN stations all over the world. Every one of those bases cost millions of dollars in the 1940s and 1950s. That's billions of dollars today! In Alaska we are talking about 50 bases in the middle of nowhere and each one of those bases needed hundreds of people to build them! That's the money that made Alaska! That's why Anchorage grew so fast. There were millions and millions and millions of dollars – cash, mind you, cash! – going into Alaskan pockets between the Second World War and the Earthquake. There was money running in rivers down the streets! The economy in Alaska today is puny compared to then. You think the pipeline boom of the 70s was big?! It was chicken feed.

Even more important, there wasn't anything like direct deposit and IRS agents electronically snooping. You got paid in cash. You spent the cash. If you filed tax returns you said you were broke. Who was going to prove you wrong? It was a cash economy and everybody had cash, spent cash and no one was the wiser.

To return to my story, I came to Alaska as part of a labor crew working on some of those Cold War sites. I was a cement man. Wherever I went, I laid the concrete. Not very brainy work but it paid. I was flown in with my equipment and tons of bags of cement. The frames were already in place when I got there. All I did was pour and smooth, pour and smooth. Some of the pouring was for White Alice sites and we are talking about pouring tons of concrete into frames that were three or four stories tall. I worked on sites in Port Clarence, Tin City, Attu, Cold Bay, Romanzov, Pedro Dome, Ladd Field and ended up in Anchorage working on Battery B. Battery B is the nuclear missile silo that overlooks Eagle River that everyone can see from the highway and is now called a "recreational facility."

This is all important because it gives you some idea what kind of money was rolling around Alaska. Figure that each of those remote bases cost about $30 million in those dollars – that's about $400 million today – and there were about 50 DEW, LORAN, ACW&S, Navy and Coast Guard facilities and we are into the billions. Every one of those sites required all kinds of labor on the ground and lots more men in Anchorage and Fairbanks who handled the incoming material. Sure, the military did a lot of the transport but there were bush planes galore that were clogging the landing strip in Anchorage. Keep in mind that Anchorage and Fairbanks combined only had about 5,000 people and half of them were women and children who did not work! Like I said before there was cash running down the streets. It was hard **not** to find a job. On top of that, everything was cash, cash, cash. I didn't see a check until almost 1960 and by then I'd been working the streets for five or six years. Didn't have a bank account until just before the Earthquake.

In those early days I did not want to give up my regular job to work the streets. I'd been poor too long to let good money go away. But I could only work during the summer. When the snow came I had to stop working. That's why snow today is called *termination dust*. For a *Cheechako* like you, *termination dust* is the first dusting of snow on the tops of the Chugach Range, the mountains due east of Anchorage. Those mountains over there, where my finger is pointing. Back in those days you could not work construction during the winter so when the first snow of the season dusted the tops of the mountains it was time to *terminate* what you were doing. You had six weeks to wrap-up your construction projects. Today, of course, we have *Visqueen* and all kinds of portable heating so you can work construction year-round. It's just colder during the winter but the pay is better.

I only worked construction for two seasons, 1945 and 1946, and spent the winter in Anchorage. No way was I going back to San Francisco or Sacramento or Petersburg. Besides, I had cash in my pocket. A LOT of cash. Thousands of dollars. For a boy like me that was big money. Bigger than I had ever dreamed of having. Five years earlier I was picking up cigarette butts and rolling a dozen or so into one smoke. Now I was buying cigarettes by the case! A $20 bill then was like a $100 bill today and $20 then bought a helluva lot of things.

It was in the winter of 1945 I met two men who changed my life and set me on the road to murder. They were Bernard Zabriskie and Al Fortunato. They pretty much ran downtown. Zabriskie was old even then. I don't think he was ever young. He was a druggist and in those days that meant he was the drug dealer. It was all legit. If you wanted drugs you went to doctor and got a prescription and the pharmacist filled it. There was only one legitimate doctor in town, Harold Silvestri, and he was, as they say these days, a real piece of work. He had absolutely no sense of money. Not a single brain cell when it came to finance. He was making money by the wheelbarrow load but had lots of problems and every one of those problems drained him dry: drugs, liquor, women, gambling. At one time in the 1940s he was going through about $4,000 *a month!* That's $50,000 a month today! Even my late wife couldn't go through money that fast! Where he got that money is a big part of this story and I'll bring it up later. But, for you, I have to keep the events in chronological sequence.

Anyway, I was a concrete man for about a year. That's two six-month stints in the Bush with a winter in Anchorage in-between. It was that second winter that changed my life. I was in my twenties and I was spending every dime I had on women. I was the original horn dog. I'd screw anything. I was never into drinking in the sense that I wanted better Scotch or a higher class of wine. I did drink, and drank a lot in the Marines, but my weakness was women. Any woman. That's where I spent my money. That was how I met Zabriskie in the winter of 1945. He was well into his 60s then and he took me under his wing like I was his long-lost son – or a son he never had. He was a horn dog too, even in his 60s. We were peas in a pod, he said. We had crossed paths my first winter in Anchorage but it was the second winter when I got into the altercation – what a nice word, *altercation* – with some construction workers at the Double D Lounge. The Double D, by the way, was named for the bust size of the working girls in the lounge. I was getting a bowl of chili – that was the expression in those days. A bowl of chili and a working girl cost the same, $20 – when these three plywood jockeys from Unalaska came in. They were from South Dakota and looking for a fight.

This guys had money in their pockets all they wanted to do was fight?

Go figure.

Anyway, one of them moves me along the counter and calls me a jarhead. That was fair; I was a jarhead. I was a Marine and my haircut was called a flattop. I wasn't looking for a fight so I just moved down the counter.

That wasn't good enough for one of the cowboys and he kind of swung at me sideways, flailed his arm like it was sort of an accident. I'm betting he was trying to spill my beer and then start something. I saw the arm coming in the reflection of the glasses behind the counter – the Double D didn't have a mirror behind the bar. None of the bars did. Anyway, here comes this forearm and I blocked it. I'd just spent four years on the front lines in the Pacific and I still had my hand-to-hand reflexes.

But there were three of them.

They were, at best, 19.

And from South Dakota.

If the fight had been out in the open they probably would have taken me. One of them could have come around behind and that would pretty much have been the show. But I was in the Double D and had my back pressed against the counter. I guess they figured that made the counter a fourth man. They guessed wrong. My first hit, an elbow, exploded the nose of the guy who was supposedly-innocently swinging at me with his right for arm. I'll give him credit for not going down. He stood rooted to the floor, blood all over his face. Then he tried a roundhouse with his left and I stepped into the blow. His inside of his forearm bounced off the outside of my forearm. By then I had cocked the right arm and went for his solar plexus. This time he went down.

One of his buddies, a punk who outweighed me by a good 30 pounds and was six inches taller, stepped around his falling buddy and came at me with flailing arms. This guy had never seen a day of boot camp let alone an hour of combat. There wasn't enough room to me to do any duck-and-spin move so I just kicked him in the balls. It was an easy kick because his legs were tangled with his buddy on the ground. He went down hard.

Number three was a bit of a problem. He was a short guy, about my size. But he had a knife. It wasn't a knife like switch-blade or a Bowie. It was a work knife, the kind of a blade you would keep in your back pocket on the job site, for cutting twine and cardboard. This changed the equation. The first two guys were just farm boys. This kid was serious. A man could get killed with a knife like that.

By this time I was locked to the floor. There were two boys thrashing around on the ground and my legs were tangled in their bodies. I still had my back to the counter and the third punk had jumped up and was flying toward me, the knife in his outstretched right hand. I felt the blade go through my jacket – it wasn't that warm in the Double D so I still had my jacket on –lucky me – and knew the point of the blade had found flesh even though I didn't get a flash of pain or anything like that. The blade ran down the outside of my left arm and I knew I was wounded.

It was that flash of *you are wounded* that flicked a switch in my mind. With the first two cowboys it was just a bar fight. But the instant I felt that knife find flesh, it was back to war. It was kill or be killed; no quarter was required. As much as I could I twisted sideway and slammed his knife forearm with my fist and felt the bone break. He kind of fell forward and I upended my elbow into his face and he snapped backwards. There was not an ounce of mercy there. It was me or him.

Up until that moment I didn't know that much about Zabriskie or Fortunato. Even if I had known about them I could have cared less. One was a real old guy, the age of my grandfa-ther – if my grandfather had still been alive – and the other was the age of my father – if my father were still alive. The only thing the three of us had in common was that we were all horn dogs. I didn't know Zabriskie owned the Double D and a lot of other property in town – not that I cared – and that Fortunato was his front man. I might have called Fortunato a pimp but he was a lot more than that. He was a very bright guy and a master at managing things. He not only ran the Double D but he also kept the books on all of Zabriskie's enterprises. He kept the books in his head, let me quickly add, because there was no paper involved. It was the paper that got you in trouble with the United States government. Everyone knew that and no one wanted trouble. No paperwork no investigation. Everyone dealt in cash and Zabriskie was at the top of the food chain. He converted his cash to property. That was where the big money was.

And is.

That was the way it was then. Zabriskie bought property with cash and then traded the land around. That is, he ran up a debt for, say, $1,500 and then paid the debt by selling the guy to whom he owed the money a piece of property worth $1,500 for one buck. When someone owed him big bucks, he took land. That way no money, as in cash, actually changed hands. No cash, no income. No income, no tax.

Since I went to work for Zabriskie and Fortunato pretty soon after the fight, it's important to understand how downtown operated. It's also important to my story so we'll have to take this side trip. At that time there were three different forces, if you will, that affected what happened downtown. There were the police, all four or five of them. The cops were not bad men or on the take the way the term is used now. Sure they took some freebies along the way. There were plenty of freebies to go around. But these guys were not on the take any more than cops today are on the take. Sure, there were a few bad apples but for the most part the cops were doing a decent job. That job was to keep the peace. We didn't have murders like we do today so the cops weren't running around investigating homicides.

They arrested a lot of drunks and let them sleep off the booze but we were a quiet town. One of the things that made it a quiet town were the MPs on the streets. The military took care of their own. If an airman or private got into a row, the city police would hand them over the military police and that would be it.

In those days we didn't have a court system like we do today. Today we've got federal courts and superior courts and municipal courts. There was a federal court then but local stuff that wasn't important enough for a federal judge was handled by a Commissioner. He was appointed by the feds and he acted as a judge on the small stuff, crimes today we would call misdemeanors. If you had a problem, you wanted to go before the Commissioner. He was local and things were loosey-goosey. If you went to federal court you were in for a hard time. The judges were political appointees who only wanted a name for themselves so they could get a better job in the lower states. They didn't care about the locals and worse than that, they didn't care to learn.

To give you an idea how sleazy some of these attorneys from the lower states were, the year before I got to Anchorage the United States Attorney in Juneau made the front page of the *Anchorage Times*. Now that was odd. What happened in Juneau usually stayed in Juneau but this case was just too delicious to keep from the rest of the territory. This guy was caught with $1,500 he had received from a woman who was then under indictment for stealing a trunk that contained $10,000. That would be about $200,000 today. The exchange was being made in a Seattle hotel room and the U.S. Attorney was caught with the money in his hand, green-handed so to speak. What was his excuse? Well, he said the woman was paying back the money she had stolen and wanted the U.S. Attorney to make sure the money was returned. Right. But he didn't say anything about the $1,500 in his hand that had come from the stolen $10,000.

When it came to the police chiefs, most of them were pretty good – with the exception of one. They were honest and law abiding men who spent most of their time playing politics. They had to. They served at the pleasure of the Mayor of Anchorage and mayors represented the uptown people, the big money. As long as you didn't create an uptown problem, everything was hunky dory, to use an old expression. This is not say that the mayors were crooked, some of them were, but it was an uptown crooked that rarely leached all the way down to Fourth Avenue. The uptown people came downtown, the men anyway, so we all knew the movers and shakers of Anchorage.

Actually, that's not true the way I said it. Everyone came downtown because that was where the stores were. Fourth Avenue had the hotels and stores and restaurants on the west end, from the courthouse to the water. The other end of Fourth Avenue, and Fifth for that matter, from about E to the cemetery was the downtown I'm talking about. It had the lounges and brothels. Those bungalows between C and the cemetery were The Line. I'll bet a lot of the people who bought those homes since the 1970s don't know they are living in whorehouses.

The lounges and brothels basically stretched from where that Balto statue is today all the way to C Street. We didn't call them bars in those days. They were lounges. There were some beyond C but they were pretty dumpy. The end of town was Gambell and everything beyond that was the 'flatlands.' In those days when you opened a tavern you threw away the front door key. You never closed. There were people drinking 24/7, around the clock. There were military people and construction people and bush pilots – but the bush pilots later switched to the lounges across the street from Merrill Field.

The Double D was about midway between what is C and D on the north side of the street, the side that went down when the Earthquake hit. It was well past it glory days by 1964 but just after the Second World War it was hopping. It was in a block long string of lounges where you could get anything you wanted: booze, women, gambling, whatever. There were not a lot of drugs in those days. Marijuana, yeah, it was called *gauge* and the coloreds smoked it. Musicians used a lot of it. There wasn't that much of it around and it was expensive. It was also dangerous to sell because in those days the court really put the hammer down on the peddlers. I didn't do drugs but I knew who was selling. So did the cops. As long as there wasn't a problem, the cops didn't care. We didn't see the hard drugs, heroin and cocaine, until the 1960s. Then we had drug problems.

Right after I took the shiv in the arm I got hustled out of the Double D. Zabriskie wasn't there that night but Fortunato was. Fortunato was always there. Brawls were one thing but when a knife or a gun was involved, the police got called. The last thing Fortunato wanted was a problem in the Double D. One moment I was holding my arm to stop the bleeding and the next Fortunato had me out on the sidewalk heading toward Fifth. There was only one doctor in town, Silvestri, and he was in cahoots with everyone. He asked no questions and took his pay in cash. He's the guy I talk about a bit ago whose pockets were black from burning cash. Silvestri sewed me up and that was that. He didn't ask me for any money but from what was said it was clear that the Double D was going to cover the cost.

Then Fortunato stuck me in a cab and we headed uptown, away from the lounge strip. I said I wanted to go home, and by home I mean a room in the YMCA. Hey, I was spending my money on women, not a bedroom! But Fortunato wouldn't take me home, he took me to a brothel, one Zabriskie owned. It was out of town – and I do mean out of town. It was on the other side of the landing strip, the Park Strip today, and lost among the trees out there, about where 15th and C are today. When I asked him why he was going to all this trouble he said he wanted to give the cops a chance to look for me and not find me. Back in those days the cops got the call that there was a problem and they *investigated*. I'm using *making quotes* in the air with my fingers because *investigating* meant the cops showed up, took down some names and spent a day asking questions. If they couldn't find me after a day the case went into the cold files and that was that. After those cowboys got patched up – by the same doc – they got shipped out. And I mean flown out that night. The construction companies wanted no problems. Fighting was a problem. You fought, you went home. It was just that simple. There was way too much construction money to get screwed by three idiots from South Dakota. There was even a pilot, "Gypsy" Davis, who specialized in such fly-outs, called garbage runs. He'd fly anyone anywhere anytime, day or night, rain or snow and he never talked about what he was flying. If you wanted to go *now* you went to 'Gypsy.' That's what happened to those three cowboys. The construction company they worked for didn't want any trouble. Those guys were trouble therefore those guys were gone.

The Anchorage lounges, taverns, brothels and restaurants wanted the construction workers' business but no trouble. The construction companies wanted their workers to blow off steam in Anchorage not on the job site. But a knife or gun was not acceptable. If you pulled a knife or gun in Anchorage you'd do it on the work site and that could lead to a contract being yanked. You pulled a knife or a gun, you were gone. Those cowboys were gone before I woke up the next morning. I wasn't going to have a problem because I had not pulled a knife or a gun. It was self-defense, not that anyone in the Double D was going to be talking to the cops anyway. The only thing anyone cared about was getting those cowboys gone.

I was about to argue with Fortunato until I realized that I was being stashed in a brothel. There were only three women in the house but I wasn't picky then. One was about 19 and the other two were in their 30s. I spent three wonderful days in that home, all on the house, so to speak.

There are a lot of myths about prostitution and let me tell you it is a multi-billion dollar business. That's –illion with a "b." But it's the myths of prostitution that are the moneymakers, not the reality. In reality, the actual business of prostitution is miniscule compared to the porn industry. Hookers, working girls, call girls, whatever you want to call them, are in a business just like any other businessperson. The smart ones make good money and save it. But they are only about one in ten, the same percentage as the smart lawyers, engineers, doctors and teachers. A lot of everyone gets hooked on drugs, drink themselves into legal problems, marry poorly or end up with children who drain them dry. Working girls aren't any different. Everyone has money problems and working girls are no different than anyone else. There are highly successful women in Anchorage right now who started out as call girls.

Yeah, sure, a lot of girls in prostitution end up broke. So do a lot of lawyers and doctors. Money comes and it goes. Even if you save diligently there is no guarantee that you are going to die with money in the bank. That's what Social Security is all about. It's a lot better to give poor people money then have them shoplifting food. You aren't really giving them anything, you earn the Social Security you get.

The big money in sex is the fantasy. Millions of people are paying for the fantasy – not the sex. Today, sharp businessmen and businesswomen are catering to the fantasies of sex with movies, pictures, stories, novels and on-line chat. If you wanted to get into the pornography business in the 1950s or 1960s, you had to have a product in stores: magazines, books, videos. So it took a lot of money to get into the business. Hard core, soft core, call-ins, adult movies, whatever, took a lot of upfront money to get started. Today everything is a download. All you need to make millions is a few thousand dollars and a web site. Even better if you are the investor, you can cater to the specialty market. In the old days you could go classy with

Playboy or *Penthouse* or nasty with *Hustler* or *Screw*. Today you can find every sexual kink on-line for about $10 a download. You don't need to produce videos or DVDs, no magazines, no police raids, no distribution problems. Just a web site and the money rolls in.

Selling fantasies is profitable because a fantasy is clean. When a guy dreams of messing with two girls at the same time there are all the benefits and none of the downside. In his mind he gets the girls that he wants, the bodies that he wants. He performs perfectly and then the fantasy shuts off. He opens his eyes and he is back in his office. He doesn't have to worry about lying to his secretary about what he is going to be doing for an hour during the workday. He doesn't have to worry about finding a place to park near the brothel. He doesn't have to worry about having the charge show up on the family or business credit card. He doesn't have to worry about crabs or sexually transmitted diseases. He doesn't have to worry about meeting someone he knows going in or coming out of the brothel. He doesn't have to explain any scratches, bruises or whip marks on his body at the gym. He doesn't have to put with the mucus and ooze of the human bodies or the smells that linger. He just shuts off his private browsing window, deletes what's on the download and History and he's in the clear.

I don't know what prostitution was like before the Second World War but in the 1940s the girls were the color of the rainbow. They were black and white and mulatto. Not a lot of Mexicans or Filipinos like there are now. There were a few Natives but not that many. Not that many foreigners, Eastern European and Russian I mean. It was primarily black and white ladies. Mostly from the South. Zabriskie and Fortunato ran the largest numbers. They had about ten houses with about 30 women who were always coming and going. The women were always changing. Some went to Fairbanks. Some got married. Some just ran away, got on a plane and were gone. Some went to the Bush. There were some long time working girls but not that many.

Zabriskie got his start with women in the Alaska Gold Rush town of Iditarod and never looked back. It was profitable in the nickel-and-dime sense of the term. But in those days that's where the money was. Today it's in stock and bonds and moving money but that's not the way it was in the 1940s and 1950s. Zabriskie retired with about a million dollars then; that's ten times that much today so he didn't do too badly in the nickel-and-dime businesses.

There were some specialty operations, mostly bondage, but if you wanted something really kinky you went to Seattle or Los Vegas. No one went to Portland, too prudish. Most of the girls came from the South and talked that way. That was the way it was all the way through to the Earthquake.

Like I said before, 10% of the working girls did well for themselves.

One more thing before I move on, and it is important for my story. Brothels changed from the 1940s to the 1950s. In the 1940s they were homes, as in houses, that were small and had a few girls. There were two or three large brothels with as many as ten women but they were still small operations. You went in, paid your money and spent about half an hour inside. They were called bawdy houses or houses of ill repute and about once a year one of them would get closed down. That was because some uptown women got their nose out of joint because their husbands were getting something they weren't providing at home. A couple of houses would be busted and the fine was $500 which was magically paid. The house were closed and the women who ran the homes just moved their place of operation. Everyone knew what was going on, everyone downtown anyway.

After three days at the brothel Fortunato came back and offered me a job. He liked the way I had handled the three cowboys, though I didn't even know he had seen me in action. Pay was twice what I was making as a cement man. Year round. So I took the job. Met Zabriskie that afternoon, the first time I had actually shaken the man's hand. I knew him as a horn dog because that was the crowd we both traveled in.

We were both hooked on women and he set me up to help him manage the business, his business, the bawdy houses. I'm not going to call myself a bouncer because I didn't beat people up. I just made sure that none of the women got punched or beaten. I ran money, the cash, from the houses over to Fortunato at the Double D and stood watch over the booze when it came in by barge. There wasn't a lot of violence then. That came later. But in the 1950s it was a great job. Money was good and women were aplenty.

Fortunato was Zabriskie's partner but he was not muscle. He was a schmoozer. He was good at dealing with the powers in town. He kept the books and solved the problems at City Hall and the Police Station. I was the downtown man. I did the dirty work, I guess you'd say. I didn't go looking for trouble, I just handled it when it came my way.

Depending on how you want to count, Zabriskie had a dozen *establishments*. Now he was an interesting man, fascinating fellow. There's been quite a bit written about him over the years almost all of it is based on what he said. I'd not saying that he was lying but I am saying that once he sold out of the brothel business he cleaned up his family history. That always happens. It's all fine and good to be a hail fellow well met when everyone is downtown but the minute that fellow moves uptown the last thing he wants is any link with downtown.

According to Zabriskie he was born in Russia – the original one, not the USSR – and had run afoul of the Czar's police. I don't know what he had done but in those days I guess it didn't take much to piss off the Czar. Whatever it was the Czar was doing he kept doing it and that's why there was a revolution in Russia. Zabriskie got the boot and ended up in New York where he became a druggist. He worked his way across the United States, drug store by drug store, until he ended up in Iditarod. I like the story Zabriskie told the papers but I am a l-i-t-t-l-e skeptical. See, druggist in those days were bootleggers. They could give prescriptions for alcohol and that's how they made their living. No one made money on drugs the way we know them today. If Zabriskie had been born about 1880s, which he said he was, that made him 20 in 1900 and 26, a grown man, when the Pure Food and Drug Act passed. Penicillin doesn't get discovered until about 1930 so from 1900 to 1933 Zabriskie was a legal drug and alcohol pusher. That was probably the way it was though he never said it that way. I shouldn't be too harsh on him; it was legal and what he was doing was legal. But whatever it he was he was selling, he had to move frequently so I suspect he was selling something that upset local folks. Not alcohol, though. Prohibition didn't start until 1919 so he would have been 40 by then – and in Alaska. In Iditarod. That town went from boom to ghost in about two years. Word around Anchorage was that he was selling more than drugs and booze. He started selling women. Nothing wrong with that.

He bounced back to the lower states and then to Juneau and finally to Anchorage about 1925. Booze was illegal then. That was when Anchorage was a real frontier town. Funny thing about frontier towns, they are only frontier towns downtown. For most folks *downtown* is anywhere between Main Street and the docks. Or, in Anchorage, the train station. That's sure the way it was when I got here, three blocks of lounges, brothels, gambling parlors, pawn shops and cheap restaurants along one side of Fourth Avenue and the nice stores on the other side. We were not that big so our sleazy downtown wasn't that large. Just three blocks long. Behind the buildings was a vacant swatch of forest four blocks deep all the way to the Alaska Railroad yard.

Anchorage was the biggest town in Alaska but we were still small. Small when compared with the cities in the Lower 48. We had a population of about 40,000 in 1960 but we were growing out of our britches by 1964. But in the 1940s we were city on the move and by that I mean the money was here! That was when things began to change from frontier to boomtown.

The late 1940s were a boom time. In *Alaskanese*, that meant that everyone who wanted a job could get one. We also had a mayor with an adjustable value system, John Manders. He was the right wrong man for Anchorage at that moment in our history. He had come north for the worst all reasons. Worst, that is, if you are uptown biddie. He had been a lawyer in San Francisco when he went into the drinking and stealing business. When he didn't have the money he needed to drink he just dipped into the probate accounts at his law firm. He drained one account dry before they caught him. His drinking and driving led to the death of a man whose family sued him for big bucks, about half a million in today's dollars. He declared bankruptcy and left town. That's how he ended up in Anchorage. Even better for me, Manders was a horn dog like me so everyone along the lounge strip knew him well. His wife did not like Alaska so she fled back to San Francisco and never came any further north than the Golden Gate Bridge. That left him free to do whatever he wanted in Anchorage and did he do a lot!

More important for Anchorage at that time, he could have cared less about all those crazy rules of the lower states. If you wanted to do business in Anchorage, that was good and he didn't care about things like permits and inspections. He didn't care so his staff didn't. So the police didn't. No one had time to worry about the niceties when there were millions of dollars of construction projects in Anchorage and ten times that much in Bush projects with every nail, inch of wire and cement bag coming through the city.

Even more important, every dime that was earned in Anchorage rolled around in the city. You earned your money in Anchorage and you spent it here. That was your only choice. So the money earned just rotated from a workman's pocket to the working girl to the shoe store to the electric utility to the bank where it went out as a loan to the company that had paid the working man in the first place. Around and around and around the money went and everyone got a piece of the pie. Then there was the military money and the liquor money and the road construction money. It was boom time like no one had ever seen before and everyone knew would only last a decade. Manders was no fool. He understood exactly what a boom meant. He and Anchorage were riding a financial juggernaut and who was he to slow it down?

So he didn't.

He also made sure his staff and the police got the message.

But with the town growing so fast there were plenty of problems. With so many men – and so many of them horn dogs like me – and so few women the natural outlet were the prostitutes. I know; that was my business. With the military and construction industry employing almost exclusively men, there was a real need for women – and lots of them. Manders' attitude was that prostitution was good for the city's economy, it kept men from being belligerent and what the hell, if it worked for him why not everyone else? So every man was getting his bowl of chili and the police didn't care. What was the problem?

Well, the problem was that the military did care. That was probably because some of their corn-fed boys were coming back from town with the clap. So, since the City of Anchorage in general and the Anchorage Police Department in particular did not seem to be expending much energy in resolving the problem, the Brigadier General issued the city an ultimatum: solve the prostitute problem immediately.

Right. Like this was going to do anything?

The general wasn't saying anything new. Everyone knew there was a problem with prostitutes. But nobody cared. But the General appeared to be serious. He sent Mayor Manders a letter stating that unless the situation was cleaned up he would declare the entire city of Anchorage "off limits" for all troops on Fort Richardson.

Like this was going to make a difference. A lot of his men lived in Anchorage. If they had families, their wives and children lived in Anchorage. Everyone from the base was buying food in Anchorage. Everyone from the base was buying shoes and shirts and pencils and nails from Anchorage stores. Remember, Anchorage was seeing about 60 new residents *a month*! Every new person needed everything and there was only one place to get it: downtown.

Did the Mayor take the threat seriously?

Are you kidding me?

He just left town for a few days and stuck the problem on the police. The police chief pledged the old 100% cooperation to solve this problem. Then the taxi cab drivers' association, whatever it was called in those days, passed this resolution that it would expel any of its drivers who *knowingly* took a military man to a brothel or drinking establishment.

Sure.

Cabbies are famous for *knowing* all the brothel and drinking establishments and *not knowing* who their fares were or where they had dropped them off. Anyone smarter than a clam knew this promise was going no place.

The Anchorage City Council did exactly what you would have expected it would do. They pretended to take the matter seriously. To show they were taking the threat seriously they fired the police chief which was no big deal because he was only an Acting Police Chief anyway. Then they replaced him with the man they had wanted in the first place but could not appoint because that was the Mayor's job.

But the Mayor was out of town.

It was all so convenient.

But on paper the City Council looked like it was doing something.

Then the new police chief did exactly what you are supposed to do in a case like this: you show a lot of motion but no movement. The police raided the bawdy houses and arrested a grand total of *nine* women suspected of having a venereal diseases and transported them NOT to the city jail but the hospital. They also arrested about 30 men for vagrancy and gave them blue tickets. In those days a *blue ticket* was a one-way ticket to the lower states you didn't pay for. The lounges loved that because it got 30 headaches out of town on the city's tab.

But none of the women got a blue ticket.

Then the general did the old backpedal. Since something had been done, he could say that his threat had been taken seriously. Then he said that since the problem had been taken seriously – those were his words, "taken seriously" – he was not going to follow through on his threat to declare the city off limits. Really? The detaining of nine women none of whom went to jail for prostitution? Wow!

But there is a backdrop to this story because it involves a man who would become central to the murder you want to know about: Jack Jonstad. This little episode with the military was the first time I had ever head of Jonstad and this is where your story really begins."

Jethro Cadawalader

Being a student of history, Jethro Cadawalader was well aware of the tick of the eternal clock. He did not need someone to tell him what was going to happen. He could read the tea leaves. He also had the good sense not to open his mouth and tell the truth. He did not want to be, in his words, the modern version of Laocoön – either of them.

Leaping back in time, Laocoön, the Trojan priest of Poseidon, upon seeing the giant wooden replica of a horse had remarked that he did not trust the Greeks even when they came bearing gifts. To show his contempt for the image he hurled a spear at the offering. The spear struck the horse and produced a hollow sound – and then a groan *came from within the* bowels of the wooden animal. This, of course, should have been a very strong clue that there were men hidden inside the hollow wooden horse. But before the citizens of Troy could respond, a knot of mighty serpents sent by Poseidon and Athena or Apollo (choose your historical source) rose out of the sea and devoured Laocoön and his sons. Their deaths were interpreted by the Trojans as proof that the horse was sacred and everyone knows how this story ended.

But the legacy of Laocoön is duplicitous. One version has him and his sons being devoured for attempting to reveal the true nature of the Trojan horse. In the other version he was killed for having sex with his wife in the temple of Poseidon or, alternatively, that his wife was simply in the temple when he was making a sacrifice. Thus, in an historical irony, Laocoön was punished by the gods for either being right or wrong. Historically and mythologically interesting, Cassandra, the daughter of the King of Troy, made the same prediction. She, however, was not devoured by sea serpents.

Cadawalader was sure that the first version was probably true. Telling the truth is never without consequences; the larger the lie exposed, the greater the punishment. He had seen the combination occur too often not to recognize that truth is the pathway to disaster. Moreover, as a lawyer, he fully understood that life was, for the most part, Sethian. Once again, a student of history, he knew that one of the seminal Egyptian deities was Seth, a god in human form with straight black hair that draped to the middle of his chest. But he had the face of an anteater with ears like a rabbit that were squared on top. Though Seth was the most recognizable of all Egyptian gods, he represented the one aspect of humanity that never made the transition from the Egyptian to Greek pantheon. In addition to being the god of embalming, Seth was also the god of a concept that the West, from the Greeks to the modern world, cannot comprehend: organized chaos. The very term throws us for a loop. "Organized chaos" is a *non sequitur*, an oxymoron. If something is organized there is no chaos. If there is chaos, by the very definition of the word, it is not organized.

As both a lawyer and resident of a frontier community, Cadawalader understood the implications of Sethianism: real life was a mess. Not all good was rewarded and a lot of evil simply slipped through the cracks. You could work hard and smart your entire life and still end up in a back alley digging through the garbage for food. Crooked people did well and more often than not and in many of those cases, what goes around did not come back around. Good people did bad things on purpose. Bad people occasionally did good things. Having a heart of gold would not keep you out of the deep mud and more than a few men and women of god had sticky fingers. There was neither rhyme nor reason why inert people succeeded while more talented individuals failed. We were all in a celestial game of craps and the best that we could do was drive the road of life carefully and dodge the potholes we could see.

An excellent example in the Alaska legal profession – which was spoken of in whispers in the legal community and never at all in the Anchorage newspaper – was the Bailey Bell case. Bailey Bell was a defense attorney in Anchorage who had previously been a federal prosecutor. One of his cases involved two men who were accused of defrauding the federal government. The case was dismissed when Bell presented a letter from the primary accuser exonerating the two defendants. Only later did the judge find out that Bell had "induced" the accuser to write the letter. Everyone in the legal profession at that time knew what that "inducement" had been and not a single one of them had felt compelled to discuss it publically.

It was, however, discussed at length in the Chili Parlor, the bawdy restaurant and brothel owned by a black madam, Marie Cox. The women were $20 apiece, the same price as a bowl of chili in the Chili Parlor, and thus the Anchorage expression that a man was going to get a "bowl of chili." Marie Cox had been constantly in trouble with the police before 1950: Conspiracy, Assault and Battery, Aiding and Assisting in Procuring a Ticket for Transportation for a Prostitute, Keeping and Setting up a Bawdy House, Buying, Receiving and Concealing Stolen Property and Receiving Money from a Prostitute. Then, after 1950, when she opened the doors of the Chili Parlor and lawyers, judges, police officers and members of the Assembly gathered in her dining room, she disappeared from the legal blotter. At the same time, the Chili Parlor became the place to go to "resolve matters" before they made it to court. If you could not negotiate a settlement in the Chili Parlor you were not trying very hard.

After the judge discovered that Bailey Bell had "induced" the accuser to write the letter which terminated the case, the judge had what half a century later would be called a conniption fit.

He was not going to be made a fool of so he filed charges of intimidating a witness against Bell. But he could not try a case which he had initiated so the matter was dropped into the court of Anthony J. Dimond, the man for whom Dimond Boulevard is named. By accident or design, it was a bad choice. To a man, the lawyers and judges in the Chili Parlor agreed it was by design but not a word of that universal conclusion exited the glass doors of the establishment.

Dimond was as Alaskan as one could be in 1952 when the case came to his attention. He had been Alaska's lone delegate to the United States Congress from 1933 to 1944 and had been a wizard at selecting juries when he was in private practice in Valdez in the 1920s. In one particular suit against the Kennecott Copper Corporation in which a worker was maimed, Dimond managed to have the jury packed with men who had lost legs, arms, fingers or eyes. Even the judge was crippled. When it came time to address the jury, Dimond, who had himself been crippled during the Gold Rush when he nearly blew his leg off, limped before the jury to plead the case of his client. The jury found for Dimond's client "without leaving their seats." That phrase from the newspaper instantly became an Alaskan legal expression and was oft used when discussing Dimond's legal prowess.

Later, the attorney for the Kennecott Copper Corporation remarked to a friend that "Justice is not only blind, but she's lame also, in Valdez anyhow. Next time I try a damage case against Dimond I'll take care to have every maimed man in Valdez kidnapped in advance of the trial." That too was frequently quoted to young Alaskan lawyers studying for the Bar.

Dimond was as slick as they come. He dismissed the charge against Bailey Bell on a technicality: the specific section of the United States Code at that time – Title 28, Section 451 – had inadvertently left out the word "Alaska." Though "Hawaii" and "Puerto Rico" were specifically mentioned, "Alaska" was not. Dimond therefore ruled that Alaska courts were not federal courts and thus lacked jurisdiction. In other words, Bailey Bell was not guilty because of a misprint: justice Alaskan style!

Cadawalader knew the line between good and evil, so to speak, was very fuzzy in those days. Decades later everything would be squeaky clean and it would be hard to stray because the paper trails were miles wide and had cyber depth of both time and space. But in the 1950s all of Alaska was still the Wild West. As an example, one of the Chiefs of Police, A. R. Winston, had *business relations* with Marie Cox along with one of the most dangerous men in town, Z. E. Eagleburger. Eagleburger had been convicted of murder in Wyoming and after spending more than 10 years in prison he wanted to fall off the grid.

So he came to Alaska.

And it did not take him long to drift back to his old ways. Within a year of his arrival he simultaneously opened the Frontier Bar in Palmer and the Green Lantern in Anchorage. Neither was a bar; both were very high stakes gambling establishments. He and his partners were busted a couple of times and once he went on trial for Assault with a Dangerous Weapon. But after he and the Chief of Police began having business dealings, he didn't seem to have any more legal problems.

But there was a new world coming and it did not take a rocket scientist to know that. All anyone had to do was read history. Everyone knew the fences of civilization were going to come in; they just didn't know when the barbed wire would actually arrive. The other thing Cadawalader knew for sure was that when the fences came in there was going to be absolute chaos as the old timers tried to keep doing things the old way with the smart operators figuring the new angle. Frankly, a lot of people were surprised that the civilizing hadn't come sooner. But it was coming and in a big way.

It was in June of 1950 that everything got very Lower 48ish. At that time just about every lounge, tavern and bar in town charged the same for drinks. Wherever you got beer it was the same price. Uptown, downtown, out of town the price was the same. That was the way it was. Prices were fixed for beer and

Black Russians and Manhattans. It was the same in every other industry as well. It didn't make any difference if you wanted to buy a hammer or five sheets of plywood, four shirts or two pairs of trousers, a set of dinner plates or a dozen light switches. The prices were the same all over town. There was certain logic to the price fixing. As long as all the businesses were charging the same price for the same item then the merchants could concentrate on service. If the price was the same, what distinguished you from your competitor was service.

Which was crock.

Price fixing is illegal because it eliminates competition. Every Economics student knows that. The way you get better prices, better service and better product is through competition. What the Alaskans were doing was just gaming the system.

Until June of 1950 the feds didn't care. Then the boom got lowered. Just about every industry was hit with federal charges for price fixing or, in the words of the indictments, that the individuals collectively and individually, were guilty of a "conspiracy to raise, fix, and maintain arbitrary and noncompetitive prices and uniform terms and conditions in the sale of – (insert the product and name of the industry here) – to consumers in Anchorage, Alaska and vicinity." The trials lasted about a year and were incredibly expensive. Every member of the Anchorage Bar had a client and those lawyers who had ethics – and, yes, there were lawyers with ethics – told their clients the same thing: "You cannot beat the federal government. Admit your guilt, pay your fine, change your way of doing business. There are some battles you cannot win. This is one of them." Those clients who listened survived; those who fought the feds ended up with legal fees they could not pay and still went out of business.

It was at this moment that downtown went from bedlam to maelstrom. Prior to June of 1950 Anchorage had been a handshake town. Other than property records, people didn't do business on paper. They cut their deals and lived up to their word. Everyone was paying property taxes of some kind but no one was paying the IRS. That was because nobody had any paper-work. No paperwork, no paper trail, no proof of taxes owed, no taxes paid. Everything was cash and cash made no enemies. Correction, come June of 1950 it made an enemy of the IRS. That was when it was revealed that the IRS really didn't need paperwork. The agents just showed up and figured how much you owed. For that year. Then the agents multiplied that year by seven, as far back as they could charge for back taxes.

By 1952 Anchorage was a different town. The wild and wooly days were over. Zabriskie knew it and bailed on the city. He could read see the shadow of the future starting to fall. He knew what was going to happen when the feds began demanding paperwork. Once they figured out on paper who owned what, he was going to be hit with a massive back tax bill, large enough to close down everything he owned.

But you cannot snooker a guy like Zabriskie.

No matter how smart the feds were, Zabriskie was a step and half ahead of them. He knew that no matter what he did the trail of all the money he had been making was going to lead back to him. So he cut the feds off at the pass. He sold everything to his long-time partner Fortunato. Fortunato was just as sharp as Zabriskie; he knew what he was doing. He had colon cancer and was not going to be around much longer. He also had a young wife. If it wasn't planned it sure worked out pretty nifty. Zabriskie sold out to Fortunato for a dollar – called income – paid his tax on that income and left for Seattle. Zabriskie walked away clean and when the IRS seized Fortunato's property for taxes and back taxes, all they got were the structures. Fortunato had already legally transferred all of his assets to his wife. He died in 1952. The IRS got zip.

But there were the only two of the very few who escaped the federal assault.

Before June of 1950, Anchorage was basically run by two dif-ferent groups of people. They were small groups, but they did what they wanted. Uptown was run by Elston Randolph, presi-dent of the largest bank in town. He kept the lid on the social people and stopped the fat matrons from starting an anti-saloon league. It was actually quite easy because he was the owner of the largest bank in town. That was his grip on the uptown crowd. He controlled the big money and he could make your life easy or hard, it just depended and a lot of big people jumped through some awfully small hoops but ended up pretty well. That banker was a horn dog is in own right but he was a bit more sophisticated about it. He had a woman on the side and kept her in style. His mistress shared a home with her mother and Randolph visited when he felt like it. Everyone knew what he was doing and no one cared. But then the bodies started dropping out of the trees and life got very expensive for him.

Word was that he got drunk one night and killed a man, the first drunk driving accident in the history of Anchorage. It was a hit-and-run and shortly thereafter a guy without a car appeared out of nowhere and said he was the dirty dog that hit the old timer. He got a light sentence and a few years later, out of the blue, he got a sweetheart deal with Randolph's bank. Word was that the Chief of Police also did well. But the bodies kept coming. Randolph's mistress decided to get married and shortly thereafter her new husband supposedly committed suicide. Story around town was that between the night the man was supposed to have committed suicide and the day that the coroner's jury found for suicide, about half a million dollars changed hands. It was a good bet that Silvestri got a good chunk. He was the only established doctor in town and it was his office that had performed the autopsy. It was right after the coroner's jury that he started spending himself broke, thousands of dollars a month.

Downtown the undisputed emperor was Zabriskie. But he was not your typical despot. He didn't run rackets the way Cordova Benson would. Zabriskie was simply the go-between when someone downtown had trouble uptown. He and Randolph were joined at the hip so nothing really big happened. Every once in a while a bawdy house would get raided and it would make the newspaper and that made the blue-noses happy. But fines were paid and things went back to normal fairly quickly. Business was business.

As Zabriskie was leaving and Fortunato was dying, Cordova Benson from Trenton, New Jersey appeared. One day he was just there. None of the lounge strip owners had a clue that someone of his ilk was coming much less that he was a symbol of the new age. But from the moment he arrived everyone knew that a new page in the history of Anchorage had been turned.

Benson's entrance was dramatic. He walked right into the Anchorage Downtown Retail Liquor Dealer's Syndicate board meeting and told the astonished collection of distributors and lounge owners that he was taking charge. He was going to handle all *difficulties* relating to liquor distribution and sales, gambling, prostitution and drugs. Every outfit in town was going to be paying for that service on the basis of their income. He expected moneys to be paid monthly starting the next January and made it clear that payment was not optional. Even the yokels in Anchorage knew this was nothing more than extortion.

No one believed him. They knew they were going to be paying protection money but there was nothing they could do about it. That was because he had a rather large ace up his sleeve: local muscle. He had teamed up with the one man on the strip whom everyone feared: Eagleburger. Everyone knew Eagleburger had friends in very low places and those friends frightened the lounge operators right down to their bootstraps. Eagleburger was also in bed with the Anchorage Police Chief so everyone knew there would be no help from the direction. Benson had closed off all the exits. Thus did the lounge owners come to realize that Anchorage had indeed entered a brand new world.

Jack Jonstad

With the blessings of hindsight it is now easy to understand what Jack Jonstad was. Historically, in those wild and heady days just after the Second World War he was discounted as nothing more than a shill – and a seedy one at that. But while he was being lambasted as sleazy and disreputable by the liquor-and-gambling establishments of that era, he was quietly building a bridge to a future he saw coming. It is not known if he was in contact with the forces that were to reshape the lounge strip after 1950 but if not, he certainly took advantage of the moment. He may not have been a haruspex but he could read a crystal ball better than any traveling circus fortuneteller. Whether by accident or on purpose he was able to maneuver himself into the right place at the right time and from the end of the Second World War to the 1964 Earthquake he stripped the apple tree of opportunity bare.

To the outside world, Jonstad was a cypher; he was impossible to comprehend. He personified the term. What he had been doing before June of 1950 seemed to have no connection with reality. After June of 1950, his machinations became clear and he was reviled for his duplicity. In a nutshell, he inveigled his way into the good graces of the Anchorage Downtown Retail Liquor Dealer's Syndicate only to sell them out. At the same time, the party to whom he sold the Syndicate – the

Trenton, New Jersey mob known colloquially along the lounge strip as the Jerzies – trusted him no more than he trusted them. But they were all in the money-making business together and money, like politics, makes strange bedfellows.

The mighty hammer of civilization came to Anchorage, Territory of Alaska, in June of 1950. Overnight Anchorage went from a wide open frontier town to a bonafide community with rules and regulations that businesses had to actually follow. In the wake of the price fixing investigation came the IRS and thereafter an archive of acronyms identifying heretofore unknown federal agencies each with its own mind-numbing red tape and paperwork.

On the flipside of governmental organization was the clandestine world of the lounges, taverns, brothels and gambling parlors. The underground world had never been organized before June of 1950. Thereafter it was, courtesy of Jerzies who saw opportunity in the chaos. They, in the form of Cordova Benson, distilled the chaos into a lucrative money stream. Benson was the collector; Jonstad the front man. Jonstad became the public face of this new era, the go-between, the man who kept the money machine operating. He was the conduit between the old timers who would not deal with an Outsider and the newcomers who needed an ear in the police department or city hall, an organ Benson did not have. Benson made sure that the monthly fees were deposited in the local banks from the lounges, brothels and gambling parlors and Jonstad kept everyone as happy as they could be made to be. It was a new age and none of the old timers liked the new rules but until they sailed off to ports unknown, in this world or the next, Jonstad was the pebble in their collective boot.

That being said, it was the muscle that changed the lounge strip from independently operating entities into a well-oiled, East Coast dominated money machine. What made it different was that the muscle was both local and out-and-out scary.

Jonstad had been unknown to the newspaper reading public before July of 1945. He had been a long-term resident of Lime Village where it was said he had overstayed his welcome. Native villages have traditionally been understanding of non-Natives who appear unexpectedly and become members of the community. It goes without saying that such individuals have very good reason to keep a low profile and many become the responsible citizens in the Bush they never were in the large city. Whether he was excised from the village or left on his own accord, he arrived in Anchorage in the middle of the Second World War where he found employment in the construction business. Too old to be drafted, he learned to be a carpenter on the job. That did not go well and even as Anchorage and Alaska were swept into a building boom, Jonstad could not find work. Considering that anyone who knew which end of the hammer hit the nail for Jonstad to be unemployable speaks volumes as to his talent as a craftsman.

To make ends meet, Jonstad incorporated himself as the Anchorage Merchant Patrol and offered his services to the Anchorage Downtown Retail Liquor Dealer's Syndicate as a man who could solve vexing problems. Basically, it meant he was being paid to drive certain unsavory individuals out of the lounge business. This was a belling the cat job. Everyone knew what had to be done but no one had the wherewithal to do it openly. Only sub-rosa. Frankly stated, there was an enemies list of operators who were giving everyone else a bad name. Rather, they were drawing undue attention to rank and file lounge operators who were playing by the rules. The rules, that is, which were tacitly acknowledged by the Anchorage Downtown Retail Liquor Dealer's Syndicate.

It had started as a mutually beneficial arrangement. The bad boys in the lounge business found their enterprises subjected to unusual scrutiny by the Anchorage Police, municipal inspectors and federal regulators. Their deliveries were delayed, their cargo from the Lower 48 waylaid and their working girls subjected to health inspections by "Evil Alice" Powell. Powell was the sexually-transmitted disease inspector in those days and she had the power to quarantine working girls who showed any signs of venereal disease. While she could not be bought she did respond to reports of the disease when such were brought to her attention.

For his part, Jonstad never seemed to want for an income. He was not living on the hog but he was comfortable. This was known as a fact because he was one of the few Alaskans who actually paid an income tax. It was speculated that he had run afoul of revenuers in a previous life and knew what to expect. Truth or no, he was correct. When the IRS made its appearance in the early 1950s, businesses and individuals who had never paid any income tax were socked with "estimated back taxes." Jonstad was audited and paid no fine.

He came to the attention of the newspaper reading public in July of 1945 when it was announced that he would be paired with the recently deposed Acting Chief of Police, P. J. Kalamarides, to form a quasi-legal vigilante association to ferret out violators of civic ordinances. This new company would, according to the *Anchorage Times,* "conduct private and insurance investigations in addition to private patrolling."

You did not have to be a Ph. D. to know what was going to happen next. Jonstad was going to drag the unsavory operators out into the open and Kalamarides was going to use his influence with the police and city hall to come down hard on the transgressors.

Everyone was waiting for the first shoe to drop.

They did not have to wait long.

Two days after the pair had formed their organization, Jonstad entered the Plantation Club, an enterprise run by an unsavory individual by the name of Harry Gottschalk. Jonstad was, in the words of the *Anchorage Times,* "masquerading as a woman in wig, high heels, sheer stockings and all other appropriate accessories." There he "arrested Harry Gottschalk on a charge of possessing and selling intoxicating liquor without a license." Gottschalk apparently had a hard time believing that a woman was arresting him whereupon, again in the ink of the *Anchorage Times*, Jonstad "removed his wig, and to the astonishment of unsuspecting onlookers who were unaware of the situation, he lifted his skirt high and produced a revolver from the pocket of men's pants." Jonstad claimed to be a Territorial liquor license officer, a job title that did not exist, and arrested Gottschalk. In spite of the questionable manner in which it was made, the U.S. Commissioner upheld the arrest and sentenced Gottschalk to 60 days in jail.

The word had now gone out that the firm of Kalamarides and Jonstad were serious about cleaning up the city of the unsavory members of the profession. What was clearly significant was that the pair was doing it the right way. They were combining the street smarts of Jonstad with the political know-how of Kalamarides. Given enough time they might have succeeded and driving out the bad operators.

But there was a problem: you cannot have an organization that plays both sides of the same street. The joint venture of Jonstad and Kalamarides was doomed because it was a mixing of business with politics. What is good business may be bad politics and what is good politics can be bad business. What Jonstad was doing sub-rosa could not survive the spotlight in the *Anchorage Times* or the Commissioner's Court. What Kalamarides was doing required a step-by-step collection of items called evidence which, before June of 1950, did not exist. The link between the two men disintegrated quickly. Kalamarides went on to other ventures while Jonstad tried to return to his former haunts and habits.

Six weeks later Jonstad struck again. But this time he was clearly out of his depth. The tag-team of Jonstad and

Kalamarides had worked well at the Plantation Club because Gottschalk did not have a friend in town. When Jonstad tried the same tactic at the Alta Club he ran square into the power structure of the city. Worse, the police chief was not only on the take from the Alta Club but was financially linked with several of the regular patrons who gambled therein. Everyone knew that the Alta Club was a lounge fronting for a gambling parlor and many of the gamblers were prominent Anchorage citizens. Jonstad never made it through the front door. The police chief was waiting for him on the sidewalk and promptly arrested him, jammed him into a conveniently available taxi cab and sent him across town. So much for that raid.

It was no secret that Jonstad was doing the bidding of the Anchorage Downtown Retail Liquor Dealer's Syndicate even though he was not on their books. For most of the lounge owners this was fine and dandy because the removal of the less reputable operators meant more business for the rest of the taverns. It also meant that the lounge strip would continue to stay below the radar of the *Anchorage Times* because there would be fewer raids and arrests. As long as the bawdy house busts and tavern raids were out of the downtown area that was good for downtown.

But there was still a problem. In every industry, above board and under the table, there are individuals who are so disreputable and dangerous that they will remain untouched. Most unsettling these individuals usually have powerful connections which insulate them from exposure and arrest. The *quid pro quo* is so horrendous that it is only discussed in hushed terms both uptown and downtown. These are the individuals who do the truly dirty deeds. They are the Murder, Inc. of every industry and community, people who are called upon to do work that is so despicable no one will talk about it.

It was thus not surprising that the one establishment that Jonstad should have raided and everyone hoped he would raid was the Green Lantern. If there was any one lounge where everyone was sure that felonies were being planned, it was the Green Lantern. Billed as a lounge it was actually a high stakes gambling establishment and sophisticated salon. The opening ante at the poker tables was $100 and the unnamed salon featured exotic women who rented by the evening only. The establishment was owned and run by Zoria Eagleburger a man well known for taking the piss, an English expression meaning to take an unfair advantage of a situation. Eagleburger was not a man to slight. In December of 1918 he had shot an unarmed man in an illicit poker game in a room over a theatre in Wyoming. The victim was unarmed and had his hands raised in surrender when Eagleburger shot him in the stomach.

After Eagleburger had completed his prison sentence he relocated to Anchorage. Here he quickly became the heavy in town and his close associates were Marie Cox who ran the notorious Chili Parlor and A. R. Winston, the Chief of Police. Before Winston became the Chief of Police, the Green Lantern was raided with as much regularity as the other lounges. After Winston became the Chief of Police, it was not raided at all and the only time Eagleburger's name appeared in the public record was when he was arrested for assault by a policeman who did not know he was under the protection of the Chief of Police. The case went away and shortly thereafter the arresting police officer transferred to the Seward Police Department.

It was widely but quietly rumored that Eagleburger has been the gunman behind the *alleged* suicide of an Anchorage police officer who had married the mistress of the president of the largest bank in town. No one knew for sure what had actually transpired except that shortly after the marriage the husband had become a police officer and four days later he had –*allegedly* – committed suicide. The autopsy was conducted in the offices of Dr. Harold Silvestri – who became quite wealthy the next week. Within a matter of months, several members of the coroner's jury also became substantially financially flush as well. As did Zabriskie. Though no one was sure exactly what had transpired, it was clear that a lot of money had changed hands over six-day period and it was not in the best interest of anyone's health to ask any questions.

It later turned out that there was a very good reason for Jonstad not to step anywhere near the Green Lantern. While many believed it was for the good of his health, what later transpired was that it was because Jonstad and Eagleburger were in cahoots with Benson.

If there was any one thing one could *not say* about Eagleburger it was that he was stupid. He had his fingers on the pulse of crime in America and it was through him that Benson made his entrée in the lounge industry. Eagleburger was the muscle behind Benson after he arrived. The Jerzies may have been frightening figures along the New Jersey Boardwalk but in Anchorage, Benson was just an out-of-town troublemaker. Alaskans have traditionally been quite tolerant of human oddities but there is a threshold to that forbearance. Once that threshold has been crossed, troublemakers have a tendency to disappear, sometimes with a blue ticket and other times courtesy of black powder magic.

That being said, homegrown miscreants like Eagleburger are in a class by themselves. They have wormed their way into the uptown and downtown crowd and cannot be excised out. They will only leave when their patrons are gone. Thus was Eagleburger doubly blessed after June of 1950s. He was inextricably linked with the Chief of Police and the old timers on the lounge strip as well as with the Jerzies when they made their entrance. For the moment he was a man who had his feet planted on both sides of the River Styx. But he needed a shill, someone to keep him one step removed from public scrutiny. For the old timers he had Zabriskie. For the Jerzies he had Jonstad.

The world changed for the Anchorage Downtown Retail Liquor Dealer's Syndicate in June of 1950. From that moment in time the feds made it clear that price fixing in any, all and every industries was not going to be tolerated and the message came with a heavy hammer: the IRS. The United States government was digging the fence postholes and the IRS was stringing the barbed wire that would be stretched across Alaska.

However, those who study history knew that with every advance in civilization there is a corresponding sophistication on the flipside of the coin. As the law enforcers became more diligent the law dodgers will become more adept at avoiding the bureaucratic red tape. Now, instead of having no books, lounge owners kept double books: one of paper to show the revenuers and one of brain matter that could not be audited. Others issued tokens instead of cash for services rendered. In Alaska these tokens were known as *bingles* which were honored as cash along the lounge strip and in many downtown stores. It was a brilliant scheme while it lasted.

The Double D, for instance, gave a dollar bingle for an American dollar. As long as patron was spending bingles he was not *legally* spending United States dollars so there was no reason to track the exchange. Over the course of a week that one dollar bingle might be used to buy a beer, become part of a bartender's tip, pay a portion of the bartender's room rent, used to pay the landlord's electric bill, be a dollar of a loan payment to a bank and then, finally, returned to the Double D for an American dollar. The only cash that was involved was the one American dollar that the Double D got in the first place which was a wash because the Double D had to buy the bingle back from the bank for a dollar. So, on the books, the Double D took in a dollar and paid out a dollar for each bingle so no money was made and thus no income tax was generated. Multiply this one bingle by thousands and it is easy to see that the lounge strip could be a tax-free money making operation because on paper no money was being made. Bingles were also a good deal for the bartender because if he were paid in bingles, he had no income of American dollars so he did not have to any income tax because he had no income. Use of bingles also cut the income tax burdens of the landlord, the electric utility and the bank. The IRS called the use of bingles counterfeiting but they could not get everyone and a lot of the lounge owners were in their 60s. Besides, if the *dba* was in their name and their wives had the money in their names, what was the IRS going to do?

Another trick to thwart the IRS was to transfer the old *dba* to an octogenarian with a bad attitude toward the United States government and get a new *dba* under another name. Or forming a holding corporation held by another holding corporation which was owned by yet another holding corporation *Ad nauseam* and let the alleged income of the lounge ooze upwards through the maze of *inc.s* knowing that the IRS would have to go to Alaskan federal courts to pierce the corporate veil. A stack of five corporations could stall the IRS for at least a decade and by then, who knew if the original lounge or owner would still be in business or even alive?

The more sophisticated tavern owners – and the younger ones – turned to lawyers and accountants. You cannot swim against the current of regulation so you don't; you sail with it and tack to your advantage. The rules change and you change with them or pass from the scene. Those lounges that wanted to survive into the next decade cut a deal with the IRS for back taxes and moved on.

But this was not the only change on the lounge strip. There was so much money coming in from the military and construction – and going out legally through the sale of booze and illegally through prostitution, gambling and drugs – that Anchorage should have been a prime target for organized crime. But it had not been. This was not because it was so small. It was because it was so far from *anyplace* and, most particularly, because it was so hard to remove the actual cash. Protection money extorted in the Meadowlands, by comparison, could be swallowed locally or washed by businesses large and small in New Jersey. Once clean, the money could be exported to Florida legally. Or driven across the state line. Or put on a Greyhound bus or airliner in a suitcase.

But in Alaska there was no food chain of enterprises to wash the ill-gotten gains. Thus any cash raised would have to be exported unwashed and this was extremely risky. The population of the Territory was so small that everyone knew everyone else. Thus it was a foregone conclusion that anyone suspected of leaving the Territory with unwashed money would have his person and luggage searched by the feds. Any crime in the Territory of Alaska was a federal crime and that carried hard time. You could certainly make money in Alaska but getting it out of the territory was the kiss of death.

But 1950 offered a window of opportunity for organized crime. Military and construction money were flooding every street, the police force was purblind, the IRS was small and not yet effectual and less than a handful of FBI agents had to handle all federal crimes in the Territory, an area 1/5 the size of the Lower 48. What tipped the scale in favor of organized crime was the sudden appearance of the single missing link in the illicit money puzzle: an entity that could wash the money.

No one knew for sure what happened next but there were enough significant pieces of the puzzle on the table to surmise what came to pass. The president of the largest bank in town had a mistress who got married and suddenly the newly-wed husband committed suicide. The death was quickly swept under the carpet and over a short period of time, six days, a handful of people closely associated with the death became well off. Two of those people were the Chief of Police and the only registered doctor in town. It was quietly speculated that that Eagleburger had been intimately involved in the matter. It was a logical conclusion as he was the only man in the lounge and tavern business who had any experience in gunning down an unarmed man. He also had nothing to lose by providing such a service to a banker. While he may have received money for his services, far more valuable than the instant remuneration was access to the bank's ability wash massive amounts of cash. This, it was speculated, was the impetus for the sudden arrival of the Jerzies. Further, once one bank began to wash money, the rest of the banks in Anchorage followed suit. After all, it was profitable and the way the Jerzies had designed the system, it was legal.

Shortly thereafter Jonstad made his second high profile appearance. This time it was in a new partnership. The visible partners were Benson, Drochester and Eagleburger. Once again, Jonstad was back in business. Clearly having a cohort on the top side of the law had not been lucrative. Having three on the underbelly along with several banks was sure to prove a lot more profitable. Jonstad established an office in, of all places, the newly-built Zabriskie-Silvestri Building at the corner of Fifth and E. It was a block from the lounge strip, across the street from the most exclusive and profitable brothel in the city. It was also appropriately placed. The lounge crowd had long known that the land beneath the structure had been the banker Randolph's means of getting money to Zabriskie and Silvestri without the scrutiny of the IRS. The land was bought and rebought six times before the unexpected, questionable death of Silvestri in 1954 – and the IRS may never have been the wiser.

It would have made a great work of nonfiction if the partnership of Benson, Jonstad, Eagleburger and the various banks in town had suffered through hard times and been forced to put down occasional insurrections among the lounge strip owners. This never happened, primarily because of the unique circumstances of the arrangement. Jonstad had an innate ability to know just how much protection the lounge strip could pay. Drochester handled the nuts-and-bolts of crowd control. Eagleburger knew that he had stay within the bounds of his fear factor. That is, everyone knew what the man was capable of so he never had to follow through on the vague threats that Jonstad made. The bankers stayed at arm's length – an attribute of their DNA – and the police and legal establishment remained purposefully, blissfully blind to the arrangement.

One of the pages of Anchorage history that will never be completely written will be the devilish cleverness of the Anchorage banks in this era. Over the decade and half, from June of 1950 to the Earthquake of 1964, they were able to orchestrate the extrication of themselves and the lounge strip from the clutches of the Outside organized crime – at a profit! It is a tale that will never be more than a quarter-told because so many who were involved are long dead and the documents so scattered – or purposefully missing. Allegedly linked, the Chief of Police who was partnered with Eagleburger dropped off the public record for a decade and next appeared in San Diego in 1960s. Zabriskie left Anchorage in 1953 and died in Seattle in 1965. Silvestri died mysteriously in Anchorage in 1954. Eagleburger left for Arizona suddenly in 1956 and Jonstad vanished in 1964. Cordova Benson was found dead of gunshot wounds – depending on which documents you view – in the collapsed remains of the Empress Theater during the cleanup of the Great Alaska Earthquake of 1964. With these players gone, the story of their collusion went into the dustbin of Anchorage history.

Dora Whitcomb

"Oh, yes, indeedy, I knew what Harold Drochester was. Is? He's still alive? Really? Well, don't make no difference now. He's got to be in his 90s and I ain't that far behind. He's in Alaska and I'm here in a hospice in Phoenix so there ain't no chance we're gonna meet by accident.

Harold Drochester! Goodness that was a long time ago. Sure, sure, I knew him. He was the man, as we used to say. He was the man about the house. I ain' ashamed of what I did when I was young. That was what I had to do. I was a religious woman then and I sure am one now. I may not have been doing God's work then but I wasn't giving the Devil his due neither.

I got to Alaska in nineteen and fifty-five, about ten years before the Earthquake. It was tough getting to Alaska in those days, especially if you were a working girl. That's what they called us then: working girls. Nice name. Same job as down here. But you could make a lot of money as a working girl in Alaska. There was lots of money to be made in those days. There were military people and construction people and all kinds of businessmen. Lots of money.

We drove up the highway up through Canada into Alaska, three men and eight of us girls. Those men weren't pimps. They were the drivers. Twice a month trips. Those three white men had to be drivers 'cause moving working girls across a state line was strictly illegal. We were in kind of a caravan, three cars with three white drivers, four black girls, two Mexes, a Lithuanian and some crazy woman that who did not speak English at all, a Puerto Rican or Filipino. Brown not black. We were all gonna make money. We did. I saved mine; that's why I could retire.

Anchorage was a wild place back then. There wasn't any such thing as night. During the summer it was light most of the time and we were loaded with construction workers. Night time we worked in shifts. Didn't make any difference if the sun was up or down we was working. We didn't make that much money from the house but did we rake in the tips! Everyone had money then. Money to burn. Nothing like Birmingham and the farmers. They was all black there. In Anchorage, nobody cared what you were, just what you could do.

Harold was running the houses then. He had a string of them, five or six depending on the year you's talking about. String of a dozen working girls, more or less, a lot of us coming and going all the time. It wasn't like Anchorage was the end of the line. Those who left had cash in their pocket, a lot more than they was making in the lower states. That's what we called 'em, the lower states.

There wasn't really an operation in Anchorage like there was down here in the lower states. We always did things differently in Alaska. Work was the same but the pay wasn't. A lot better and like I said, the tips were great.

But you wanted to know about Drochester. He owned the houses and ran the houses. He collected the money and a lot of times brought the men over. No surprise there. A lot of on-the-house when I was younger. Not so much later. But we all got paid.

It was a dicey time then. A lot of the girls weren't that bright. They didn't see things, if you know what I mean. There are some who see the world as it is and some that don't have an inkling of anything beyond the tip of their nose. Most people are that way, you know. They go to work, whatever that work is, and finish their shift, go home and watch television. Don't know what a newspaper is. Can't read. Or won't read. Think that improving yourself means knowing who Angelina Jolie is or watching a reality show. Got a lot them here at the hospice, hope to live to the season finals if you know what I mean.

I was different. Then and now. I knew what was going on. Couldn't do anything about it but I knew what was going on. Drochester was the man with the houses but he had lots of partners. I call 'em partners 'cause he had to pay 'em. I don't mean the electric company or the grocery store either. I mean men like Cordova Benson or whatever the hell his name really was. He was out of New Jersey and spoke like it. Did not have a clue what he was doing in Alaska and never went much further south than 9th Avenue. That was where the landing strip was.

What did he look like? Typical grease ball, I'd say. Greek, Italian, Portuguese, I think. I don't know. Short, stubby, greasy black hair, the kind of man who had to pay for his women. Don't know what women in New Jersey like but I'd bet he had to have money hangin' out of his pockets to get a woman there. Sure wasn't going to get no one with his looks. Probably the reason he was in Alaska. Kind of looked like a monkey when he got mad which was all the time. He was always mad. Not yelling and screaming but like he was about to jump up and down and yell obscenities. That's the kind of a guy he was.

Nobody liked him. No reason to. Even worse than that, he was a dead man walking. Problem was, he knew it. But there was nothing he could about it. He'd pissed away his money and his well was running dry. He couldn't stay in Alaska, couldn't go back to wherever the hell he had come from in New Jersey and didn't have the money to retire. He was stuck in Anchorage. Then, just before he could have made a lot of money, he ends up dead, d-e-a-d cold letters dead.

I heard a lot about what happened before I got to Anchorage but the names didn't mean anything to me. What I got was old stories which were kind of like new stories if you know what I mean. No? OK, let me explain.

Whether you are talking about uptown or downtown there is always a group of folks what's in charge. Sometimes it's one person with a lot of muscle and other times it's a group of folk who just let the word pass as to what's what. Downtown you have to use muscle because everyone's looking for an angle and there is always someone taking the cream. When I got to Anchorage the downtown muscle was Benson and a guy named Jonstad. He was what was left of the old downtown people. But there was a lot of changing and if you had brains you could see it happening right before your eyes. Benson and Jonstad were being squeezed out. They might have been powerful back ten years earlier, say after the war, but by nineteen and fifty-five they were having problems. It was money, course, always is, and the problem wasn't going to be getting any better any time soon.

Yes, yes, yes, I know. You want me to talk about Drochester. I'm getting there. He was part of the sourdoughs who'd been in Anchorage for a while. He wasn't one of the power folks but he was connected if you know what I mean. He knew everyone and was trusted by everyone, uptown and downtown. He knew all the right people uptown and the wrong people downtown. Never carried a pistol but he knew men who did.

If you had any brains at all you knew what was happening in Anchorage. The big money was gone by nineteen and fifty-five and things were settling into the way they was everywhere else in the lower states. The big tippers were getting fewer and most of our clients – we called 'em clients – were workaday men. Lots of single men and more than a handful of married men. The usual crowd, just like Birmingham, 'cept most of them were white. Once upon a time the big money had been downtown along the lounge strip, Fourth Avenue from about G to A. Some places in the flatlands beyond Gambell but that was a rough area. If you were looking for a fight, that was the place to go.

But by nineteen and fifty-five the action was along both sides of the landing strip. That's how far the city had grown. The money was in land then. War was over, 'course, and all those remote military sites had been built so the war money and big construction money was gone. But everyone knew there was another boom coming. The Cold War was still on and Alaska was seeing more and more military folk. Economy was stable and America, hey, the fifties were a great time to be alive! Everyone had money. Except Alaskans. We were doing well but we weren't doing great.

But everyone was looking forward to the next boom when-ever and whatever it was gonna be. Drochester certainly was. He had a banker friend who was using him as a front. The banker'd sell him a piece of land for a dollar and then buy it back for $1,000 cash but put a dollar on the bill of sale. That's the way it was done in those days. You traded land back and forth for a dollar on paper but cash under the table and the IRS couldn't do a damn thing about it.

But Drochester was one clever fellow. He knew the game in town. Took the cash he got from the banker and sank it into more land. That way he had lots of land and no cash on the books and was dealing with lots of banks, not just one. Knew what he was doing. And what he was doing must have pissed the IRS off to no end. But it was legal. Harold got cash and spent it on land and took the write-off. Probably still owns lots of land in Anchorage but at 90-whatever it ain' going to do him that much good.

After I had been in Anchorage for about five years it became clear that Benson was in very deep trouble. See, and I don't know for a fact but I sure picked it up, the big boys in New Jersey were not getting what they had five, six years earlier. There had been big bucks coming in from Alaska in the 1950s but by the 1960s the well was drying up. Worse than that, the banks that had been cleaning the money had moved on. The next big money switched from land to oil and coal. That was where the big money was going to be. Not downtown along the lounge strip.

Drochester knew that was where the money was so that's where he was investing his cash. He fronted for some bankers and they slid him in as a partner on some oil deals, one hand washing the other. He came with the cash and the bankers dropped it into land and oil investment. It was no sweat off their noses: it was free money all the way around. Drochester was buying land with some of the money and investing in oil companies so either way the money was not income. He got pieces of land and oil company stock which cost him nothing. He was simply the link between the downtown payola and the bankers. That was the way it was: the lounge strip paid and the money went right uptown.

While Drochester was doing well, Benson was being washed out to sea. He was collecting less and less from downtown and fewer dollars were getting into the banks to be washed. Worse than that, the bankers were making inroads with the big boys in New Jersey. In other words, the bankers were slowly cutting Benson out of the deal. The New Jersey boys knew it but there was nothing they could do about it. Then, come 1960 and the new Attorney General, Robert F. Kennedy, money got harder to hide. I learned that the hard way because I got caught with a lot of cash in the bank. The IRS did not care how I got the money; they just wanted their share. I didn't have any receipts so I paid a chunk of the money for back taxes. Since then I've kept good receipts.

What I heard was that by 1961 or 1962 the New Jersey family was very worried about its Alaskan money. Sure, Alaska was a state, but it was still a long way from New Jersey. It was hard to get money back to the lower states. The IRS was watching bank transfers and the feds knew whose luggage to search. You could drive to the lower states but you would have to go through Canada which meant you would be searched going into Canada and then again going back into the United States.

Let me tell you, the Canadians were no slouches when it came to digging through your suitcases and automobile trunk! They were looking for drugs and they opened everything! The United States border people were pretty ruthless too.

So the bankers and the big boys in New Jersey cut a deal of sorts. The bankers washed the money by putting it into land. Then things got sticky. Now here is where you have to listen real careful 'cause this is the beginning of the end of Cordova Benson. The New Jersey big boys went along with the land scheme for a number of reason. They had a man on the ground in Anchorage, Benson. They also had some muscle left. And they had paperwork. But these three were problems. The New Jersey boys just didn't know it yet. They weren't local so they didn't know the game had changed.

Yeah, there had been some muscle a few years back but that was gone. 'Cept the Jerzies didn't know it. The heavy, a guy by the name of Eagleburger, had quietly slid out of town. He could see that the end of his empire coming fast so he took his money and ran. Or the bankers maneuvered him out, I don't know which. But he was gone by the 1960s. The old power along the lounge strip, a guy named Zabriskie, had moved to Seattle and he was gone. So the muscle that the Jerzies thought they controlled was one man, Jack Jonstad. Problem was, he had the biceps of a jellyfish. He wasn't even any good as a collector. When that Eagleburger guy was in town, yeah, Jonstad collected his dues but once Eagleburger was gone, the lounge owners slowly stopped paying their dues. When Benson came around, yeah, they paid up, but not Jonstad.

But the Jerzies didn't know that. They knew that cash was going down but they probably thought it was because of the economy. Besides, they didn't care. They weren't really paying Benson because he was getting a cut from what he collected. And they weren't getting what he collected because it was going into land and they weren't expecting to get that money

– money, as it cash – out of the land for a while. To them it was an investment in the future because there was too much risk getting it out then. So the Jerzies weren't expecting any money soon and were counting on muscle that did not exist.

Then one day Jonstad just vanished. And I mean vanished. It was not as though he had said he was leaving town and then one day he did. He just disappeared. That was back at about the time of the Earthquake. I distinctly remember that Drochester had a meeting with him on a Thursday – or it could have been a Wednesday – and Drochester had money for him. It wasn't much, a few thousand, but it was more than Drochester had been paid in a while. Harold said he was going to meet with Jonstad – as kind of an aside, not that he told me specifically he was going to meet with Jonstad – and then he walked out of the Crystal Baths. That was where we were working, the Crystal Baths, at about 5th and C, if that still exists today. We *really* cleaned you at the Crystal Baths.

I don't want to make you think that there was anything special about that day. It was just a day. It was only a special day to remember because Jonstad disappeared about that time. He never showed up to work again. He just locked the door to his office in the Zabriskie-Silvestri Building and that was that. His car was in the parking lot at his rooming house, he hadn't taken a plane out of Anchorage and no one ever saw him again. It was just poof and he was gone. We called it GDBM, 'God Damn Black Magic.' He just disappeared.

This was, like, 1964. I know for a fact it was 1964 because it was just before the Earthquake and we were dancing to the twist taking off our clothes in the Crystal Baths to *The Stripper*. It was just after breakup because Drochester was wearing rubber boots. He didn't wear rubber boots 'cept during break-up. Jonstad just disappeared. No body, no clue, no crying wife. Nothing. Just gone. I don't think anyone knew what happened to him.

But we all knew what happened to Cordova Benson."

A. R. "Ray" Winston

While it is certainly true that one bad apple can spoil the barrel, people are not apples and they do not live in barrels. A better old saw for Anchorage in the late 1940s was that that crows come in murders and ravens unkindness – and there was nothing more murderous or unkind then Chief of Police A. R. "Ray" Winston. Though his tenure was brief it was tumultuous.

Winston arrived in Anchorage at the best of all possible times for a person with an adjustable value system and his tenure was catalytic for a selection of profligates who saw nothing wrong with milking the law for a profit. He was the bridge over a River of Styx with prosperity by intimidation on one shore and profit by murder on the other.

Like many other renegades from the lower states, Winston had very good reason to choose to come to Alaska during the Second World War. He had an even better one to leave from where he had come. His port of exit had been Ceres, California where he was had been convicted of forgery – while he was a police officer. The exact details of that charge and the consequences thereof have been lost to the sands of time but suffice it to say he made his first appearance in the Territory of Alaska in Ketchikan during the Second World War where he served as a lieutenant in the local police force. He either did not tell the locals of the transgression that caused him to move north or they did not ask. It was most likely both as the United States was in the middle of a ferocious war and able-bodied men willing and able to face down drunk crabbers and belligerent halibut fishermen were few and far between.

But it did not take long for his old ways to catch up to him. Within short order he had been forced to resign. As he could not go south, he went north to Anchorage where his alleged 18 years of law and order experience got him a job at the Territorial lockup. It was the ideal place for a man whose view of the criminal justice system was rooted in the Middle Ages. Whether he inherited the medieval hoosegow or created it is unknown. What is known is that the Anchorage lockup had three times the prisoners it had been designed to accommodate. The prisoners were packed like sardines and fed – according to the complaint filed with the Governor – a stale roll for breakfast and "a cup of so-called coffee" in the evening. The prisoners were frequently beaten with night sticks and one prisoner had been killed, his body left on the floor of his overcrowded cell for almost a day before it as removed.

His stint at the jail did not last long and Winston was soon patrolling the street. In January. For a man from the Central Valley of California, Anchorage must have been a shock. While Ketchikan was a city of rain, about 200 inches a year, Anchorage was a city of snow and subzero temperatures. From October to March the Mercury bounced between 8 below and 8 above and it was not uncommon for the city sidewalks to have snow berms as high as a man. Winston may very well have felt that Hell had indeed frozen over.

But he was about to get the best break in his life.

Early in the morning of January 6, 1945, while Anchorage was asleep, 82 year old sourdough Charles A. "Bert" Bryant was struck and killed by a "dark sedan" in a hit-and-run accident at the corner of 5th and F streets. It was the first hit-and-run in Anchorage history and only the second one in Territorial history. It was estimated that the car was going about 35 miles an hour – unbelievably fast for travel on snow-covered streets even half a century later – when Bryant was hit. Anchorage was a small town in 1945, about 6,000 people, and there were very few cars – and even fewer "dark sedans."

Two weeks after the hit-and-run, Vernon Samson, a man who supposedly owned a "cream colored" car admitted his guilt. Samson was fined $2,000 and the case closed quickly. Shortly after his conviction Johnson and his wife borrowed $15,000 from the Randolph bank and within about a year the loan was allegedly paid off. During the same period, A. R. "Ray" Winston went from patrolman to Police Chief.

In spite of the fact that Samson had admitted to the act, it was generally believed that Randolph had been driving the car and Samson was simply a highly paid patsy. Randolph had a frigid wife so he stored his mistress and her mother less than a block from the site of the hit-and-run. Randolph had a son from the liaison and a hit-and-run would have exposed his paternity. The combination of the two secrets would have ruined him financially as well as socially. So a patsy was found. Or, more likely, Winston found the patsy. It made no difference. From the moment of the impact, the fortunes of Winston and the Randolph were, for better or worse, inextricably intertwined.

For a handful of years Winston's fortunes rose dramatically. Courtesy of his close association with the president of the largest bank in town, he shared in the blossoming prosperity of Anchorage. He received a prime piece of land for a dollar and constructed a home built on a foundation of sweetheart equity. He swapped other lots back and forth at a dollar a pop and pocketed money under the table or, at the very least, below the IRS radar. Just as important and lucrative, he was able to walk both sides of a very dangerous street. On the uptown side he had his hand in the pocket of the wealthiest man in town and all the prosperity such an arrangement could reap. On the jungle side of the avenue he was cavorting with madams, gambling den owners dodging the very law he represented, lounge lizards and at least one murderer. He was indispensable to both sides of the street and a conduit between the two because the city's population was exploding exponentially while the police force was only growing numerically.

But he had a genetic problem. A bowtie on a rogue only makes him a rogue with a bowtie. Reprobates who can mutate their DNA rise to become bankers, judges, ministers and even governors but the process of is one of destruction. As one oozes upwards one must slough off old friends of convenience and leach onto and into a higher class of rapscallions. If one cannot rise above his roots, he will never bloom any fuller than his birthing soil will nourish.

Winston was never able to rise above the quagmire of his past. Within a year of becoming the Chief of Police he was charged with two acts of assault and battery. The cases lingered for several years because he was, after all, the Chief of Police. By the end of his second year as Chief so many policemen were submitting their resignation that the Police Department had become the punch line of local jokes.

The act that set the lounge strip talking in hushed tones about murder for profit occurred in the early morning hours of November 27, 1946 in a house at 624 F Street. Anchorage Police Officer James T. Foley, who had only been married for three weeks and a police officer for four days, allegedly committed suicide. It has been his bad luck to marry Randolph's mistress. The speedy autopsy of the police officer was overseen by Silvestri who was receiving moneys from both Randolph and Zabriskie. A coroner's jury was quickly convened and just as quickly rendered a verdict of suicide and that, as they say, was that.

But few were the denizens of the lounge strip who could not piece together the likely scenario. Randolph was more than unhappy that his mistress had become married. The logical solution was to have the groom disappear from the scene. That was hardly going to happen while he was alive. So extraordinary steps had to be taken. The groom had been a policeman in his hometown of Greely, Nebraska so he had been convinced by Winston to become a patrolman. It was a set-up. As to who actually pulled the trigger, it was quietly speculated that it was most likely Eagleburger, a man who had a track record in such endeavors and for this particular act of homicide he would be paid. The previous homicide had netted him no income but a decade in prison.

No one had the juice to suggest any scenario other than the official version of the incident. So no one did. But everyone on the lounge strip kept a wide swath of real estate between themselves and Eagleburger. Silvestri was spending madly so he was welcome as he swept to from brothel to tavern to gambling parlor to lounge to brothel and around again at all hours of the day and night. Zabriskie and Winston profited as well. Even better for Randolph over the long run, his mistress and their illegitimate child immediately headed south. She had clearly connected the dots. Her departure was rapid and she disappeared from the history of Anchorage instantaneously.

That winter was the zenith of Winston's career in Anchorage. He had the mayor and the only convicted murderer in town in his pocket. He was the Chief of Police. He was a landowner and pocketing cash from land sales in his bank account and stuffing his wallet with payoff boodle. He had his wife and son on the Anchorage Police payroll and no one could tell him what **not** to do.

His euphoria lasted less than a handful of weeks. In January of 1947, eleven of 16 policemen submitted their resignation *en masse* – including his own son. The incident that generated the mass resignations occurred at 8:30 am on the morning of January 30, 1947 when Winston summarily fired officer Harry Prator. When Prator was slow to respond, Winston shoved Prator out the door of the police station and then followed the man onto the sidewalk. Then, as the *Anchorage Times* reported, "in full view of many persons on their way to work," Winston physically confronted Prator by pulling a "gun out of his [Winston's] holster on Fourth Avenue" and challenging Prator to do the same. Winston was probably lucky that Prator refused to draw as Winston's gun "snagged on his belt and fell to the ground." Prator then resigned from the force as did 10 of his fellow officers. With no one left to patrol the streets, Winston resigned at noon.

There was one final indignity for Winston. Now that he was no longer Chief of Police, he discovered the verisimilitude of the expression that you will inevitably meet the same people on your way down as you met on the way up. One of those whom Winston had met on the way up was V. B. Wakefield, a hotel owner. Winston had demanded Wakefield pay protection money which Wakefield declined to do.

"I wouldn't pay him off," Wakefield told the press. In response to his refusal to pay the protection money, Winston raided the hotel "without a warrant" and carted the guests of the hotel off to the police station for questioning. When Wakefield complained, Winston "offered to take off his badge and coat, step outside and fight Wakefield 'man to man.'" On the day of the raid Wakefield had 28 guests. By the next week he was down to three or four. Wakefield thus claimed $8,000 in damages: real dollar losses of $4,000 and another $4,000 in punitive damages.

Everyone of importance on both sides of the street knew that it was only a matter of time before Winston left Anchorage. He was no longer the Chief of Police and there was no other job for a man of his caliber. He sold his home to Eagleburger and Marie Cox, the structure becoming a brothel shortly after he left town. His exit was graceful and he certainly left the north-land with more money than he had arrived with.

The departure of Winston left a sizable power vacuum in downtown Anchorage. The proceeding police chief was able to lure the patrolmen back on the job but he was unwilling to reach into the tills of the lounge strip clubs. This was fine with the lounge strip clubs because it meant one less hand scooping out cash. But Eagleburger was not to be denied a patron. He could smell the money but now that Winston was gone he could not touch it. Zabriskie was winding down his career and wanted less and less to do with the nuts-and-bolts of keeping the lounges in operation, particularly as he was getting nothing for the effort. The only card Eagleburger had to play was Randolph but to play that Ace the stakes had to be appetizing to a man worth millions. It was then that Eagleburger reached into his past and contacted a prison buddy, a man from New Jersey who was connected to the Trenton mob. Six weeks after Winston left town, Eagleburger and Randolph had a new partner: Cordova Benson.

Jerry "Slick" Prendergast

" **S** lick" was a bookie. This was back in the days when "slick" and "bookie" were reputable terms. Not that "slick" and "bookie" were ever reputable terms in the eyes, or at least the vocabulary, of many people in Anchorage before the Earthquake. Stated with more geographic preciseness, the repute of the terms "slick" and "bookie" depended upon which side of Sixth Avenue one worked. To the south, from the plank sidewalk of the four-block commercial strip from C to F streets and then south to Seattle 2,000 miles away, the terms were combined to personify a person with greasy black hair, a heavy thumb, a notebook full of numbers and a vocabulary of mind-numbing statistics who made a living by knowing the outcome of a contest before the news reached Alaska. North of Sixth Avenue to the ends of the earth, that same person was slick because he read all manner of sports news and would take bets on matches, games, contests and races so far ahead of the event that there was no way he could cheat.

(It should be quickly added that Juneau, between Anchorage and Seattle to the south, was the seat of government – Territorial and then State – where "slick" implied the type of legislation therefrom and "bookie" the remote chances of such legislation being financially beneficial to anyone making less than $100,000. To the north, the communities of Fairbanks and

Nome had been founded on the prestidigitations of man and Mother Nature. Fairbanks had been originated by an embezzler who subsequently absconded with every dime in the city while Nome had been founded on the bet that you could sluice a year's living between high and low tides four months out of the year.)

Being a bookie in Anchorage was a daunting task because of the warping of the concept "here and now." In the rest of America, rather, the rest of the world, gambling is predicated on the belief that the term is a singularity: gaming money won is paid immediately and where the bettor is standing. Further, a great portion of the joy of gambling is being present as the contest is unfolding. Having a bet on the outcome while one is watching the game enhances the experience; betting on the Packers playing the Eagles and not being able to watch the game has all the thrill of reading Plato. But from Alaska that involvement was four time zones away from the action and the fastest communication in 1950 was via a telephone system that had yet to be upgraded since the days of Alexander Graham Bell. On top of that, communication from Alaska to the lower states was expensive, unreliable and prone to disruptions by man, wind, rain, snow, ice, equipment, sun spots and sleepy Canadians.

Further, the most reliable source of information were newspapers and magazines printed in Seattle. If such came by plane they were known by the Alaskan term "Air Fresh." This meant whatever it was had just come off an airplane from Seattle – along with a ton of crispy vegetables, yet-to-be-frozen steaks and unsalted mackerel. Everything else was called "cold storage" which meant it had come to Anchorage by truck either cold – as in eggs – or frozen – as in vegetables. Sometimes the trucks carried Second Class mail, like magazines, and these were also referred to as "cold storage" meaning the news was not "Air Fresh."

By hook and by crook, mostly crook, Prendergast had made a science of the primitive communication system that existed in Alaska right after the war. He and a legion of similarly minded entrepreneurs in the lower states had created a pastiche of communication lines that could get gaming results to Alaska in not-quite-real time but faster than "Air Fresh." The electronic travel of gaming results in the lower states was quick and convenient but once the electronic pulse encountered the Canadian border things got a bit sticky. Simplistically stated, there were a number of intertwining systems of electronic communication. There was the United States military system which was a line-of-site microwave tower arrangement which worked well as long as the weather was cooperative which, in Alaska and across Canada, was the most uncooperative weather belt in North America. Then there was the so-called civilian communication system which was hard wire – when the wires were up, when the power grid was active, when there was personnel to operate the system and when the Canadians were not asleep in the operations rooms. Then there were the telegraph and teletype networks as well as local phone lines and service. Complicating the matter, none of the systems were standalone operations in the sense that all military traffic went only by microwave or all civilian calls went only along hard wire to the lower states and into the national communication grid. Depending upon exigencies, communication could hopscotch from civilian to military lines with no consideration as to jurisdiction and, from the long lines carrier point of view, the cost of such communication. To keep peace within the Alaskan family, the United States military came to a financial agreement with the long lines carriers. Basically stated the military assumed that a certain amount of military communication would travel over private lines and compensation was reasonable. The private communication which traveled over the military communication system was conveniently ignored even though it was well known that such traffic was extensive. It was assumed, anticipated and predicated that this comingling of resources would be resolved with the replacement of all communications systems at some convenient time in the future.

From the point of view of the feds, Prendergast wasn't even small time. His clients were Anchorage residents only for the simple reason that he paid in cash. You had to see Prendergast – in the visual sense – to get your winnings. No one had bank accounts in those day so you made your bets in cash and got your winnings in cash as well. He took no bets over the phone lines outside of Anchorage so, if you happened to be on a remote military base and wanted to make a bet, you had to do so through an intermediary in Anchorage. Using the military communication system for the making of bets on the remote bases was a guarantee of disaster because those lines were monitored. They were also 100% owned by the federal government which took a dim view of its communication system being used for gambling.

From Anchorage to the lower states, until the money was available for separate, stand-alone military and civilian communication systems, Prendergast was free to use whatever means of communication was available to conduct his business. Taking full advantage of this opportunity to mix-and-match communication systems he was able to establish a cadre of associates using the military system to speed gaming results to Alaska faster than the civilian lines. This made him the most reliable bookie in town and thus sobriquet "Slick."

Geraldo Sandro "Wop" Andretti

"When I was told I was going to go to Anchorage, Territory of Alaska, I thought the boss was goosing me. I mean, Anchorage middle of F&^%ing nowhere!? Polar bear and penguin land? Eskimos and igloos? Yeah, sure I was. Then he said, yeah, I was going. Today. As in right now. It was in the middle of the summer so I didn't need a winter jacket or anything like that. And, yeah, he was right, I was going to F&^%ing nowhere with Al "Big Lip" Marchetti.

This was not a plumb assignment, let me tell you. "Big Lip" was one of those guys who never seemed to get anything right. "Fat Lip" would have been a better name because that was all he was ever getting. He'd fight anyone and lose every fight he ever started. I wouldn't say he was dumb, just a little slow. No, real slow. He was the kind of a guy you'd send out for Marlboros and he'd come back with Camels, no matches and dragging six FBI agents behind him. No one ever called him a wise guy.

We got the call to go to Anchorage from "Fat Louie" Grimaldi. He'd been in some prison in Wyoming, another place in the middle of F&^%ing nowhere. It was one of those I-know-a-guy-who-knows-a-guy-who-knows-a-guy kind of deal. "Fat Louie" spent ten years with this guy who ended up in Anchorage. Called about this opportunity with lots of bucks. "Fat Louie" knew the man, Eagleburger, wasn't pulling a fast one. He was right about that. I worked with Eagleburger for five years and he was not one to lie when it came to money. He knew where the cash was and how to get it. He was muscle but not like you needed it in Anchorage. He was a lone wolf type when it came to the dangerous stuff. Had a small group that could break heads when it was necessary but he was the most dangerous man in town.

The money was there but he needed us. We needed him too. Beautiful relationship. He was easy to work with as long as you stayed on his left side. You left his right side alone, right arm. Had a thing for his right arm, hand. It wasn't like he had a gun in his waist band. Just a quirk and you did not want to rile him. Like I said, he'd killed a man in Wyoming and he popped another guy, a cop, just before "Big Lip" and I got to Anchorage. Eagleburger was not a man to cross. Easy to work with, wily with the dollars but you had to watch your back all the time.

I had been around a few blocks before I was sent up north. I'm not going to say that I was well-connected the way the term is used in the movies. That's a Hollywood concept. Everyone in the families is well-connected. The problem with working for any family is that you spend most of your time sitting around. You'd sit and wait for a call. At what you'd call a social club. All the wise guys would hang out and wait for the phone to ring. Then someone, or two or three someones, would go out to do a job. No one knew what job was coming.

I got my call in the summer of '52 and was told to meet with "Fat Louie." He was pretty old, in his 60s, which was old then. "Fat Louie" started talking about F&^%ing Anchorage, Alaska, a territory, not even a real state yet. Says that he's going to be running the lounge strip and he's sending me and "Big Lip" up to the middle of F&^%ing nowhere. Says I'll be working with a guy named Eagleburger that I could trust and a *babbo* named Jonstad that could not be trusted. We were meeting in a park so I knew this was a good gig. Hard to bug a conversation in a park. We were walking and talking and "Fat Louie" was telling me that I am to keep a sharp eye on "Big Lip." It wasn't that he was a snitch or anything like that. He was just stupid, a *cafone*. My job was to double-check the books, deal with the meat eaters and above all else, keep the banker happy. That was the first time I heard the term banker and I had to ask twice what he meant. Banker was not one of our street terms. Twice he had to tell me that the banker was a banker, name unknown, the money laundering end of the business. "Fat Louie" said that the banker was snake slippery and it was gonna take someone on the ground with brains to keep an eye on him. That was the first time anyone said I was smart. I thought I was pretty cagey 'cause I'd never been behind bars. That was the Number One reason I was sent to F&^%ing Anchorage: I didn't have a paper trail. "Big Lip" did and if he was taken out by the feds – which was not really expected to happen – there had to be a clean back-up. I was that back-up.

So north I went in the summer of '52. Stayed until '64, about two days after the Earthquake. Went up with "Big Lip" and left him there. He went down during the Earthquake. They had a big earthquake up there, you know. A real strong one. It was even big for Alaskans and they get shakers about once every few months. It was huge. Downtown Anchorage looked the bottom of a shake-and-bake bag.

I had never really been out of Jersey – a couple of trips to New York on business – not that that I had ever wanted to leave Jersey – when I got assigned to Anchorage. Best gig I ever had. Better than the next one here in Tucson. When the FBI finally shut me down in '66 there really wasn't much I could tell them that they didn't already know. By that time I was a one-man show. "Fat Louie" was gone, Jonstad was gone, Eagleburger had died that year in Arizona – the reason the FBI waited so long to close me down. Didn't take the Witness Protection Program 'cause I'd saved my money. Wasn't going to give up my cash to the U.S government! It was time for me to go anyway so I took my cash and was gone. I'm talking now 'cause there's no one left to care. The old Jersey family got eaten alive by the Russians, investigated to death by the feds and drained broke by lawyers and the IRS. Funny that I would be the guy left with the cash.

I got to Anchorage in what everyone was calling its transitional era. Anchorage was just starting to growl. It would roar later but in '52 it was as wide open a city as I had ever seen. It was a frontier city too. The only thing that was missing were the six guns. It was 2,000 miles north of Seattle and in those days that was a l-o-n-g 2,000 miles, not like today where you can jump on a 737 and be in Seattle in three hours. It was six or seven thousand people, mostly men, in a city so small you could see all of it from the top of a three-story building. But did it have money! They were building military bases all over the Territory and there was money to burn.

The lounge strip ran down one street, Fourth Avenue, from Cook Inlet to F Street. But it was an odd strip, not like I was used to seeing in Trenton. It wasn't tavern-to-tavern-to-tavern. There were all kinds of little shops in-between, photography stores, pawn shops, cafes, a barber shop. The lounges were slotted in between the regular stores and honeycombed with basements for gambling. One of the lounges, the Double D, shared a back wall with a grocery store. It had leased the grocery store storage area and removed the wall between the two establishments. Then they put up a false wall – why, I have *no* idea since everyone knew what was going on – and installed gambling devices.

Like I said, everyone knew what was going on. Everyone, e-v-e-r-y-o-n-e. Uptown people even knew where the brothels were and what the women specialized in. Like I said, Anchorage was a real small town.

I got there just as the old guard, the old fogeys, were on their way out. The king of sleaze then was Zabriskie and he was the embodiment the quote from Alaskan humorist Warren Sitka, "In every community there is always a scoundrel who buys his way to respectability. He's usually called Mayor." Zabriskie wasn't a kingpin the way we use the term today. He did not run downtown. He owned a number of clubs and a lot of brothels and when there was trouble, people came to him. He was the man with the money who paid, directly or indirectly, a lot of the bail for hookers and gamblers. If you had to get out of town quickly, he was the man to see.

But Zabriskie was on his way out. There had been a big change in Anchorage the year before I got there. The Chief of Police ran himself out of town and the new Chief was no one's fool. He was as political as they come in the sense that he knew not to mess with the lounge strip. But then again, he didn't have to; the feds were in Anchorage in a big way. For the first time the FBI had gonads, the IRS was looking into everyone's books, the revenuers were eyeballing all the liquor distributors and there were about 20 federal cases for price fixing and those cases affected every industry in the Territory – and I mean every industry.

I can't tell you that much about what happened uptown and, frankly, I never cared what happened uptown. "Big Lip" and I were downtown people and that was where we stayed. We got two rooms in the Crystal Baths, a brothel/rooming house run by one of Zabriskie's madams for about a year and then we moved to the Four Season Apartments at 9th and M. We stayed there until the Earthquake. Then we couldn't stay there because the place came down like a house of cards. It went from a six-story reinforced concrete structure to a pile of rubble in about 30 seconds. When it came down it took every scrap of paper the FBI called *evidence* with it. That's when got "Big Lip" whacked. That had been his life insurance policy. When it was gone, he was gone.

But I'm getting ahead of myself.

In '52 we were working with two locals and one phantom. I call the banker the phantom because I never saw him, never met him. I knew who he was and what he was doing for us but it's not like I went to his office. I didn't and "Big Lip" didn't either. We called him the phantom because we knew who he was and what he did but we never met with him and only talked about him as 'the banker.' That's what "Fat Louie" called him so that was fine with me. As long as the boys in Trenton were fine with it, so was I. "Big Lip" was fine with it too which was odd because he usually got involved in everything and usually messed it up good but I guess he got the word to lay off the banker.

Anyway, the two partners we had were guys named Eagleburger and Jonstad – and there was a hangeroner named Drochester. Eagleburger was a scary fellow and I can see why Jonstad did so well with him. Jonstad was grandfatherly-like. The lounge owners felt comfortable talking with him. They should have been comfortable. He had been working with them for ten, fifteen years, with the retail liquor dealer's whatever. He had been their heavy in the early days which goes to show just how unorganized they were. He got a few lounges busted but that was about it. He tried to do it legally and that went nowhere. Then he hooked up with Eagleburger and that was the link with "Fat Louie." After that, everything changed.

What really made things pop was dealing with the banker. He was the first laundry. We could not do what we were doing without a laundry. The money came in as cash but in Alaska it was not safe to take cash out the Territory. It was too risky. It was better to do something with it locally and then transfer it legally. That made it an odd gig. I didn't have to collect like in Trenton. That is, I didn't have to pick up cash from 30 or 40 lounges and brothels and drop it off. All I had to do was make sure that the cash from those lounges and brothels was deposited in the bank. So "Big Lip" and I just went around town looking tough.

Actually, that's not correct. My job was go around town and keep an eye "Big Lip." Here was a man who could burn water. He could make the simplest of tasks complicated just by being himself. And talk about chiseling! He could not comprehend the concept of big dollars. He was a nickel-and-dime man who did not understand that it was just as hard to make $100 as it was to make a $1,000. So he spun his wheels on penny ante crap that got him in trouble – and me in hot water too.

As an example, one Christmas, I think it was in '61 or '62, Kennedy was President, and I get a call from "Fat Louie." He got a call from the banker who said that "Big Lip" was shaking down the Crystal Bathhouse and Benny's Home Cooking. Both were fronts for brothels run by one of Zabriskie's madams. Zabriskie didn't own the brothels anymore. He'd sold out to a guy named Al Fortunato who died before the IRS could get to him. But somehow Zabriskie was still getting money from the brothels, I assumed through the banker who was his best buddy in Anchorage. Those two shared four murders, a lot of folk along the lounge strip knew that, and nothing binds two men together more than a few murders – and several million dollars.

Anyway I get this call from "Fat Louie" that "Big Lip" was shaking down the brothels and running a few of his own as specialty operations. I was told to stop him. That's a lot easier said than done because Anchorage was not Trenton. In Trenton it would have been easy. I'd just tell "Big Lip" to stop and that would be that. But I didn't have any muscle in Anchorage. That was Eagleburger's job and he was gone by then, living in Arizona. Worse, word on the street was that he was chirping. But if he was chirping, "Fat Louie" didn't know and if anyone would go down it would have been 'Fat Louie.' "Fat Louie" never went down; died too soon. A lot of other wise guys did but we could never pin it on Eagleburger. I think he played his own game and he must have done it well 'cause he died with money in the bank. Had a son somewhere who's probably doing real well right now.

Anyway, I told "Big Lip" to stop and he gave me this song and dance about how I worked for him so to shut my pie hole. I called "Fat Louie" and "Fat Louie" called Eagleburger and there was some stars and bats and everything got settled. At least that was what I, "Fat Louie" and Eagleburger thought. I think that was when "Big Lip" started collecting the records. He wasn't going to go to no feds but I do think he and Jonstad were in cahoots to do something. They were really hungry and by then the skim wasn't enough.

This takes a little explaining. See, in Trenton we got a skim. I'd make a pickup and take a percentage. That's how everyone got paid. It was all cash and as long as you didn't keep any paperwork it was all off the books so it was tax free. But in Anchorage we got paid through a bank account. The money from the lounges and brothels went into the bank as a deposit and we got a percentage paid into our own personal accounts. Yeah, there was a paper trail, but it was legal money. I paid my taxes and invested the money – not with the banker – and I made a nest egg. "Big Lip" and Jonstad took their money out as soon as it came in and didn't save diddly. I told 'em that sooner or later the IRS was gonna come calling. Neither of them cared. Jonstad had his mind stuck in the good ol' days of Zabriskie and Fortunato where everything was cash and no books meant no taxes. "Big Lip" had his mind stuck in Trenton where you got your money and ran. Neither of them understood that the game had changed – everywhere – and the IRS did not need books to assess back taxes and the only places where you could run and hide were places you wouldn't want to go.

In the ten odd years I was in Anchorage I saw all kinds of different ways of making money. I guess the reason I'm still around is that I understood that Alaska – and for that matter, the United States – was changing. When I got to Anchorage in '52 everything was cash and carry. By the time I left in '64, no one wanted cash. Cash raised too many issues, particularly when the drug culture took off. That was the way the feds closed down drug dealers. They didn't go after the drugs; they went after the money.

In Anchorage the banker saw this coming. He understood what was going to happen and got ahead of the curve. He'd actually been ahead of curve for a few decades, he and Zabriskie had been manipulating land ownership and land prices for as long as the two had known each other. It also made it easy for the banker because he was using the bank's money, not his own. He owned the bank so I guess you could say all the money in the bank was his. I don't think that the feds would have looked at it that way had they known what he was doing but I never read that he was ever caught with his hand in the cookie jar. Nor Zabriskie. They both died rich and respected and no one will ever know how many tax-free millions of dollars they sloshed back and forth between the two of them.

The banker also saw opportunity in dealing with Trenton. I've got to say he was as clever as they come. He put so many buffers between himself and everyone else that no federal authority was ever going to catch him. There was only one link between him and those of us on the lounge strip: Jonstad. But it did not take me long to pick up what had been happening before "Big Lip" and I got to Anchorage. Seems that everyone who had dealings with the banker ended up dead or fleeing for their lives. The crooked police chief left in about '50, two years before I got to Anchorage. Silvestri spent himself into poverty and died owing the IRS more in back taxes than J. Paul Getty was worth. Word on the street that Silvestri was killed and the men who did the deed, both doctors, walked away with a cool $2 million apiece – and both lived to a very ripe old age and never saw a day behind bars. Zabriskie left in about '53, right after I got to Anchorage and screwed the IRS out of every dime it had coming by selling out to Fortunato. Then Fortunato put all his money in his wife's name and died. He screwed the IRS out of every dime they had coming from him too. What a guy! He flipped the finger to the IRS on his deathbed and there was not a damn thing they could do about it. Eagleburger stayed in Anchorage until about '56 before he left for Arizona. Funny thing about him, he may have been gone but he was still pulling strings until the Earthquake. But he was still a very dangerous fellow the whole time I was in Anchorage. He could pick up a phone and make very nasty things happen. But I'm betting he did not want to cross the banker and being a l-o-n-g way from Anchorage gave him coverage.

I have never been the sharpest knife in the drawer so it took me a few years to understand what was what. The first thing I did was lose my New Jersey accent. Occasionally I slip, like at the start of this interview but, for the most part, I talk like I was born in Denver. I copied that speech from a construction worker who lived at the Crystal Bathhouse for a year. He wasn't a friend, just someone I listened to a lot when he was in town. He was from Denver. That was the speech pattern I matched.

Talking like a wise guy might have been good Trenton but not so much for Anchorage. Once I saw how the wind was blowing, I knew I wasn't going back to Trenton. By the time I left Anchorage in 1964 there were too many ways for the feds to go after the families. The big money wasn't there either, not the cash anyway. So when I left I went south because I was pretty much going to be on my own. I'm surprised that you found me, frankly, since I've been out of the game for quite a while.

It took me awhile to piece together what the banker was doing. It was hard to track but once I understood what was happening I could follow the money. It was not a particularly clever scheme but it was legal. Throughout the whole time I was in Anchorage the population was increasing by leaps and bounds. Federal money was pouring into the city and the one commodity that could not be flown or barged in were homes. They had to be built. What the banker was doing was setting up shell corporations for the Trenton family which would then buy raw land on square-foot-by-square-foot basis. As long as 100% of the cash less expenses was spent on buying land, there was no income. Over the years the shell corporations increased their asset base, their net worth, but had no income and therefore paid no taxes. All taxes would be paid when the land was sold.

At the same time, the banker was giving sweetheart deals to a select number of construction companies who were building homes. As long as they built on the land he selected, they got construction loans below the market rate and delayed land acquisition payments. This meant was that the construction companies were able to pour more money into construction and finish homes faster. As the homes sold they paid off the construction loans and the land acquisition. The banker then dropped the land payoff into more land so the shell corporations were making money but showed no profit. As long as the building boom continued – and there was no reason to suspect that it would not – the Trenton family's untaxed assets were spiraling upwards. They owned lots of land but had no income.

It was all very legal.

But I still didn't see how the banker was making his money.

But what I did discover in '62, ten years after I started doing my research, was that someone else had discovered the same thing I had. At first I thought it was the FBI or the IRS but I quickly discounted that possibility. Everything the banker did was on the up-and-up. The FBI and IRS looked for illegal activity, not legal enterprises – and the bank filed taxes every year. There was always the possibility that "Fat Louie" had sent someone to do some checking but the paper trail I had discovered would take someone more than a casual visit to dig out the details. That meant they would have had to stay longer than a day or two and Anchorage was a small town. I would have known if someone from New Jersey was in town. That only left two possibilities: "Big Lip" and Jonstad.'"

Rhonda Cole

R honda Cole was a ghost. Not an ephemeral collection of vapors which floats from room to room or slimes ghost-busters but a transient presence which seems to be everywhere – silently. She was the perfect secretary, faceless and seemingly without a convolution to her brain. She was as wallpaper. She was a woman of some passion because she had four children and was not Catholic, but outside of her home she was school marm conservative, soft spoken and silent as a tomb.

It is impossible to say what she could have been had she allowed her inner spirit free but such was not to be her lot in life. She was as old as Betty Friedan but eschewed the Feminine Mystique. She was a work-a-day mother in an age when women stayed home and raised children.

Her husband was a high school teacher, not a high paying occupation, and her tenure at the bank as secretary to the president was long enough for her to enjoy an enviable salary. After more than two decades at the same job, it was said that she knew more about banking than most of the vice presidents which, in reality, was actually not saying much.

Cole had a pension for silence. Even more important, her ability to show human emotions on the job had been cauterized by time, circumstance and the endless procession of individuals and busi-nesses who believed that knowing the president of the bank put you and yours on the A list for a loan of low interest and lengthy maturity. Saints and scoundrels, wastrels and down on their lucks paraded through her office on their way to the president. She announced them, took shorthand when necessary and bid them farewell as they left. She had not opinions, offered no advice, kept meticulous notes and was silent as a crypt when it came to gossip.

But then again, she had much to be quiet about. When she started at the bank as one of three part–time tellers, Anchorage had been a town of 2,500. There were no secrets. Everyone knew what everyone else was doing and talked about it from the Oyster Loaf on the corner Fourth and E to the Court House and City Hall, on the adjacent blocks. The sidewalk footage was short but there was a lot of talking space on those blocks. Cole came to be known as "Tombstone Annie" because she was "silent as the grave." She heard the gossip but told no tales. It was this personality trait – considered a flaw in a small community – that earned her a place in the president's office. She was efficient and silent. What transpired within his office stayed behind the oaken doors of the president's innermost sanctum.

One of the realities of working for the president of a bank was understanding the difference between compassion and consideration. Financial institutions have none of the former but use the latter as business bedrock. The former is known as the instigator of bad judgment while the latter is the calculated gamble a banker is expected to take. Actuarially speaking, the financial future is predicated upon actions that are derived from statistics which are rooted in economic theory that is based on the assumption that humans are rational. Thus the very foundation of the banking industry is based on the supposition that, over the long run, more people will be rational than irrational. That being said, as per H. L. Menken, "No one ever went broke underestimating the intelligence of the American public."

Cole had lived the history of banking in Anchorage. There had always been banks in Anchorage but in the early days most had been simply facades for large institutions in Seattle. Each of these banks had an office but these were small and did not handle that much cash. This was why they stayed small. Anchorage was a city that survived on cash. No one used checks. As a consequence, most business deals were either penny ante or large. Everything in-between was a hand shake or a piece of paper which could be and was, more often than not, only worth the paper on which it was written.

Things picked up substantially with the start of the Second World War because Alaska suddenly found itself on the front lines of the confrontation. The Japanese had taken the last two islands of the Aleutian Chain and there was a real fear that the enemy might island-hop its way to Anchorage. This would give Imperial forces a staging ground to invade America from the north. Just as important, with the Lend-Lease legislation of 1941, Alaska became the transit corridor for military hardware to Russia. American planes were flown to Fairbanks where they were turned over to Russian crews. The aircraft were then flown across Alaska, the Bering Sea and Siberia to the Eastern Front. To service the growing military presence in Alaska, the ice-free port of Whittier was built, the Alaska Railroad was fortified, Army bases were built outside of Anchorage and Fairbanks and a highway was built linking the lower states with the Territory of Alaska.

With the increased economic activity, banks in Anchorage sprouted like weeds. This was primarily because Anchorage was banking paradise. The military paid in cash which was spent in local stores, restaurants and lounges. Money, as in cash, from the military burned its way through the pockets of servicemen into the tills of the local businesses after which it went to the banks where it was borrowed by local businesses which purchased goods in bulk that were bought individually by servicemen and their families at the next pay period. The only money leaving Anchorage was the buying of goods from the lower states. But more money was coming in from the military than leaving for the goods and the extra money simply ran around and around Anchorage because there was no other place for it to go. This financial merry-go-round accelerated in speed, volume and spread of goods and services after the war with the construction of remote military sites across the Territory. If the cash coming into Anchorage had been a flood when the city had a population of 3,500, it was a *tsunami* five years later when the city was three times larger.

This deluge of cash came with consequences. There is a direct relationship between the volume of cash available and the magnitude of corruption. Each fertilizes the other and it was this proclivity that brought the full scrutiny of the United States government and its alphabet soup of agencies to Anchorage in June of 1950. In a matter of less than a handful of months every industry from construction to booze and shoes to nails was hit with price fixing charges. The barbed wire of civilization had arrived in the Territory.

Regardless of the rules, banks never lose. The arrival of the federal prosecutors was a windfall to the financial institutions. Now businesses had to keep track of their moneys. They needed bookkeepers and bookkeepers needed a paper trail because there was a new sheriff in town: the IRS. Cash could make it into the till but business were wary of paying their bills in greenbacks. Everyone wanted receipts and the best receipt was a cancelled check and you could only get a cancelled check from a bank. So the banks grew in size and service by leaps and bounds.

However, as Cole came to learn, there was a significant downside to this sustained spurt of growth. While the banks were making money hand over checking account over certificate of deposit, the doors were thrown wide open to fraud, forgery and other fiscal felonies. Not every check was as good as gold and there were more than a few businesses that would rather have stolen a nickel than earned an honest dollar.

Then there was the legal illegal money, an oxymoron that does not exist in the lexicon of finance. To a banker, money has no extrinsic value. It has an intrinsic value which can be placed on a spread sheet. It is not the place of the banker to question where money came from, only where it is going. The legality of the originality of the money was the bailiwick of minions of law and order and until such time as *this* money was declared to be legitimate as opposed to *that* money which was not, the bank did not have the legal option to deny anyone the right to deposit money into their account and spend such moneys – less a handling fee.

It was in the riotous days after the war that Anchorage banks generally and Rhonda Cole specifically got her first, real, big city lesson. While her employer had spent time as an accountant for a large financial firm in Los Angeles before coming to Alaska, Cole was ignorant of the devious ways of the financial world. Her hard knocks schooling had been with locals whose greatest sin was check kiting. But after the war an 800-pound gorilla entered the room. Known around town as the Jerzies, it was the first budding of genuine, East Coast organized crime in the heretofore pristine wilderness of Anchorage.

The arrival of this new world came in the scariest of forms. For the first time her life Cole had the very real premonition that her bank was about to be robbed. Through the front door of the establishment came the last person she ever expected to see in a bank without a pistol and face mask. It was Eagleburger in the flesh and he was carrying a briefcase, an accoutrement that Cole would never have imagined that Eagleburger even knew existed much less owned. Beside him walked a man she also never expected to see in a bank even to rob it: Jack Jonstad. While Cole was surprised, her employer was nonplussed; the pair was expected. Nothing warms the cockles of a banker's heart – in spite of the fact it is an occupational hazard to have one – than clean cash on the barrel head. So the three men disappeared into the office of the president of the bank. That was the last time Cole ever saw Eagleburger. But she did see Jonstad on a monthly basis for the next ten years, every third Thursday at noon.

Lt. Col. Robert B. Johnson III

L t. Colonel Robert Johnson III was a Mormon. He was not a jack Mormon or a polygamous Mormon or even a Mormon in name only. He was a true Mormon but not cut from the same bolt of cloth one would expect of man who had been raised in the fold. He was first and foremost a military man. His father, the II, had fought in the First World War and his grandfather, I, had fought in the Spanish American War. His great grandfather had fled upstate New York as a young man and fought in the Civil War. He had not been a Robert B. Johnson but he had been the progenitor of the ancestral line of warriors.

All of these Johnsons were Mormon but all were also realists. If there is any one thing that military teaches it is the inconsistences of the human being. Soul aside, there is no mistake a rational person cannot make. A good education and a sound religious upbringing will not save someone from making bad choices. That being said, all Johnsons knew that the difference between a good officer and great one is that the great one uses those beneath him to the best of both their abilities.

There was a very good reason that Johnson III was sent to Anchorage in 1947. He was on the most secret of assignments, a task with such deep cover that even the Elmendorf Air Force Base Commander did not know what he was doing. All the Commander knew was that Lt. Col. Robert B. Johnson III was to be given maximum latitude with regard to his time and there was to be no restriction as to what equipment he ordered and no record of the equipment requested, used or never returned. Further, that equipment was not limited to hand-held items but included aircraft, medical supplies, radios, clothing, weapons and parachutes.

All materiel, regardless of size or value, was to be taken to the Anchorage airport where it was placed onboard an airplane owned by legendary bush pilot and just-as-legendary closed-mouthed pilot George "Gypsy" Davis. Davis was known as "Gypsy" because he would take unscheduled passengers and/or cargo anywhere at any time for any reason and, in all cases, have no memory of any passengers or cargo – and kept no manifests.

On Elmendorf and Fort Richardson, the High Command referred to Davis by the code name "Magic." That was because they used him to make problems disappear. The military in those days in Alaska was just like the construction industry: it had humans who were problems. Or they created problems that were very difficult to resolve. These problems were usually of a local nature: beating up a Native, raping a matron, robbing a liquor store, knifing a construction worker, threatening a superior officer, being drunk with an automatic weapon or bootlegging. The best way to start to solve a lot of these problems was get the individual at the center of the controversy into a different time zone quietly and instantly.

But it could not be done quietly if the person was extracted on a military flight. Those flight required passenger manifests. With "Gypsy," the person *magically* vanished. Be they in Anchorage, Port Clarence, Fort Yukon, Shishmaref or St. George, that person had to be gone. Immediately. "Gypsy" made it happen; rain or shine, day or night, rain or snow. He was magic. When he was called, poof, just like magic, the problem disappeared. And the High Command was, of course, *caught completely by surprise* that the individual in question had vanished from his duty post.

Johnson's authority was based on the single document he carried: an open letter from the Chief of Staff of the Army – a man by the name of Dwight D. Eisenhower – which stated that Lt. Col. Robert B. Johnson III was to be given every courtesy he requested without question. If there was a matter which required consultation, the questioner was to contact Deputy Chief of Staff of the Army Omar Bradley – and only Omar Bradley and only by telephone – and there was to be no record of any such calls.

With specific regard to Johnson, his orders were specific and clear. Though he wore the uniform of the United States Air Force, a military branch separated from the Army barely five years earlier, he was to coordinate with the United States Army and only with the United States Army. Further still, he was under strict orders to complete his assignment no later than snow cover in 1958. This was because the muckety mucks at the Pentagon had been assured by knowledgeable individuals in the United States Congress that the march to Alaska Statehood would end in the early days of 1959. Once Alaska became a state, Johnson's assignment would be illegal thus he was to have 100% of his assignment – men, materiel, strategy and tactics – in place before the President signed the statehood bill. Thereafter and until the end of his career he would be a United States Air Force Colonel whose only superior officer would be whomever the Deputy Chief of Staff of the Army was at that time.

And **only** the Deputy Chief of Staff of the Army.

And his permanent place of retirement was to be Anchorage.

What Johnson could tell no one was that while he wore the uniform of the United States Air Force and was commanded by the United States Army, his real boss was a man by the name of Allen Welsh Dulles, the head of the Central Intelligence

Agency (CIA) a civilian arm of the United States government which was supposed to have no control over any member of the United States military. Further, the CIA was restricted by law from operating within the United States. As long as Johnson's task was completed before Alaska became a state, what had been done was legal. After Alaska became a state, on paper, Johnson's boss would become the Deputy Chief of Staff of the Army and he was to have no further contact with the CIA.

This complicated chain of command left Johnson quadruply vulnerable. First, he had to avoid pesky questions from United States Air Force officers and noncoms on Elmendorf Air Force. Second, he had to avoid raising any suspicions as to his true mission with any member of the United States Army on Fort Richardson. Third, he had to avoid so much as a hint that he had anything whatsoever to do with the CIA and this included letters, cables, phone calls, telegraph messages, teletypes or even casual conversations. He was not even allowed to tell the local CIA office – which was to close down in December of 1958 – that he was on the ground. Fourthly and most dangerously, he had to deal with cantankerous Alaskans who had as much a reputation for spilling beans as swilling beer.

The roots of Johnson's mission sank deep in both American and world history. The seed had been planted a generation earlier. It began with the Russian Revolution of 1917, which, in historical fact, was a misnomer. It was not a single revolution but three. The first was bloodless in February of 1917 which deposed the Tsar as the head of government. Then came the February Revolution which actually occurred in March. (The Russians were not on the same calendar as America and Europe. There was a 13-day difference.) The February Revolution established a Russian Provisional Government which lasted all of about six months. In October of 1917, November by the Western calendar, the Bolsheviks under Vladimir Lenin seized control of the government and began what is traditionally known as *the* Russian Revolution which ended in 1923.

The impact of the Russian Revolution was felt around the world and most particularly in the United States. In the years leading up the Russian Revolution, all three of them, the general view of political radicals – all breeds – was that they were harmless utopian philosophers. The United States was a capitalistic country and Americans were more interested in making money than in pushing for obscure political ends. Further, the motherland of the socialists was Russia and prior to 1917 the general view in America was that Russia was a stable monarchy with a large army ruled by an American-friendly despot. After all, wasn't Russia an American ally against the filthy Germans in the Great War?

Then, in breathtaking speed, the world changed. In February of 1917 the Tsar was out. In October the country had fallen into revolution. By March of 1918, a little more than a year after the Tsar had been deposed, Russia signed a Peace Treaty with the filthy Germans – and gave up huge chunks of income-producing territory.

And agreed to pay six billion *marks* in compensation for German losses.

So much for world revolution.

It also meant that German troops from the Russian Front were going to the Western Front and it did not take a college chemistry professor to figure out that American boys who had been on the front lines in France since June of 1917 were going to be facing more Germans because the filthy socialists in Russia had thrown in the towel.

Even more important, though it would not be widely known for a number of years, the United States Army had been receiving disturbing intelligence about the growing threat of a socialist insurrection in Russia. As Europe was girding for war, the Russian socialists had been talking with the Kaiser. Talking, as in direct communication. It was clearly in the interest of the Kaiser to have a revolution fomented in Russia because this would take Russia out of the war. While the United States government could do nothing to stop such a revolt – which did come to pass – it wanted to make sure that the virulent virus did not spread to America. To contain the political disease, the United States Army sent a contingent of 8,000 men under the command of Major General William S. Graves to Siberia. Their primary, stated objective was to keep the Trans-Siberian Railroad open and running. Their second, unstated, mission was to keep Bolshevism from backstroking its way across the Pacific to American shores.

Three decades later the United States and Russia, now known as the United Soviets Socialist Republics, were, once again, allies against the Germans. Once again, the United States had to trust that the Russians would not cut a deal with the Germans and drop out of this war as they had the last one. Even worse, every moment that the Russians were our allies, we were providing them with military armaments through Alaska. With each airplane that left American airspace and headed over Siberia, many old warhorses wondered if the United States would be seeing those same planes re-entering our air space in the next decade loaded with bombs – and specifically atomic bombs.

This fear did ameliorate with the end of the war. If anything, Pentagon paranoia had deepened and widened. In March of 1946, Winston Churchill warned that an "Iron Curtain" had descended across Europe dividing it between the "West," then known as the Free World or the First World, and the "East" known as the Second World or the Commies. The big difference now was that the world had entered the Age of Air Warfare and having troops on the ground in Siberia to stop the spread of Bolshevism was no longer going to work. If the Russians, the Commies, were going to invade America it would reasonable come via Alaska and it would be a ground assault. It would probably start with air strikes – thus the establishment of the DEW and NORAD chain of alert facilities – followed by a millions of boots on the ground.

There was going to be no way to stop an invasion of that magnitude. So the United States military did the next best thing. It planned to plant spies in the midst of the Soviet incursion zone who would be the eyes and ears of the Pentagon. To this end the military went to the spy specialists, the CIA, and struck a deal. Until the Territory of Alaska became a state of the United States, the CIA would orchestrate a super-secret effort known as the "Stay Behind Program." Unique, hardy Alaskans would be recruited in communities, large and small, to be "Stay Behind Agents." When the Russians invaded, these individuals would "stay behind" and be the human intelligence of the American military establishment. To achieve this end they would be trained in all of the arcane arts of sabotage, camouflage, clandestine communication and guerilla warfare. They would be supplied with the best equipment and supplies that the United States military had to offer and be embedded in their own communities with none left the wiser.

Johnson was specifically chosen for the task because he had no external morals. While he had his own personal, stringent moral yardstick, he was a master of justification by rationalization. He was in a very dirty world and what he was going to have to do was for the good of the United States of America and such was going to require personal sacrifices. His job was to find and train the best Alaskans and he knew – and the Pentagon knew as well – that he would be dealing with individuals who had zero love for government, any government, and this was why they were living in as remote a region of the United States as it was possible to find in 1947. They viewed rules as someone else's problems, only followed the law when it coincided with what they were doing anyway and were very likely to look at any largess from the CIA or the United States military as theirs to do with as they wished regardless of the intent of the offering. Once *in situ* there was no way anyone could predict what these agents would do because, after all, there was little you could do to them. After all, as the Alaskan expression went, Alaska was not the end of the earth "but you can see it from here."

Johnson's job was to find these deserters from civilization one at a time, recruit them with whatever means was necessary, overlook their moral proclivities, train them as best he could in the limited time he had with them while they were in town and most important, made sure they left Anchorage without blabbing. Keeping them sober, he knew, was beyond his ability but he could keep them free of civilian, military and underworld difficulties while they were in Anchorage. He did this by accompanying them in their perambulations on the bases and around town. On the military bases he was faceless but along the lounge strip and in the brothels he was a most welcome fellow because he always came with lots of money. He paid for everything and tipped well while his recruit indulged.

In an odd bit of *quid pro quo* which, again, was unusual considering the background of Johnson and perhaps the single most important reasons that he was specifically chosen for the assignment, he established himself as a man who would pay for the most elaborate of entertainments for the recruit without sullying himself with the same sin. If the recruit wanted three women at a time, Johnson found the three, paid for them, and made certain that only bodily fluids passed between the recruit and his sources of entertainment. Johnson did not indulge; he was simply present as an informational bodyguard with a very thick wallet. As long as he was paying no one was complaining.

When Johnson first came to town he spent all of one evening surveying the most likely source of trouble for himself and his recruits: the lounge strip. A veteran of the battlefield and post war Europe he had no trouble relating to the wild and crazy ways of post war Anchorage. What he was looking for were the powers who controlled the lounge strip, the acreage where he anticipated he would be spending most of his public time with his recruits. He anticipated no trouble with the police and courts because he could make a single call and have such difficulties disappear. But the world of the lounge strip was more difficult. It did not follow civilized rules.

Being a man of the world he zeroed in on the two kings of the strip: Eagleburger and Drochester. He went to Eagleburger first because nothing makes an entrance like knocking heads with the toughest man in town.

Like a scene out of a Hollywood movie of the Chicago Underworld a generation earlier, Johnson walked right into the Green Lantern, spotted Eagleburger sitting at a table with three thugs and pulled up a chair. To say that Eagleburger was surprised was an understatement. The three other men at the table turned the scar tissue they called their faces to Eagleburger to see if this ramrod man in the uniform of a Lt. Col. with a carpet of campaign ribbons on his breast was expected. When Eagleburger did not assuage any of them, one of the hulks made the mistake of reaching toward Johnson. That was an error he would not make twice. With lightning motion born of combat Johnson grabbed the man's sleeve, jerked him forward and head-butted him off his chair. It happened so fast the other men at the table did not have a chance to say anything. Then Johnson looked at Eagleburger and said calmly, "We need to talk."

They did.

Eagleburger got the message loud and clear. Whenever Johnson was with anyone in any lounge, tavern, brothel or gambling establishment, regardless of the actions of that individual, he was to be left alone. Any damages would be paid in full later but under no circumstances was anyone to intrude. It is not known if Eagleburger asked any questions but there was one thing he knew for certain. While he, Eagleburger, could only point to two confirmed kills, Johnson had made a living of it. Or, rather, he was alive because he had done it many times. Eagleburger knew he was dealing with a professional killer and after that meeting not a single recruit was harassed to any degree in any tavern, lounge, brothel or gambling establishment. Dealing with Harold Drochester was only a matter of money. Johnson simply showed up in his office and placed $5,000 on the Drochester's desk. There would be a similar delivery every year on this date, Johnson assured Drochester, as long as no one he was with was disturbed in any manner in any establishment. The word from Eagleburger had traveled fast so Drochester did not have to ask for any further explanation.

That was the way it was until January 3, 1959 after which Drochester never saw Lt. Col. Robert B. Johnson III again.

Jerry Richards

Jerry Richards was a dancer. He wasn't just fast on his feet, he was a *maestro* of the *pirouette, rulo, pique, arabesque* and the *pas de chat*. He could be *allegro* or *adiago*. He could dance on air, dance up a storm, dance at your wedding or dance to a different tune and he was never out of step. He could not afford to be because his was the dance of death. The fancy footwork he did was not with taps or slippers but with land titles. He was Randolph's property manager and had to be the master of the *amague*, the fake move, because both he and the banker had three very scary sets of eyes looking their collective shoulder: the IRS, the Trenton mob and Z. E. Eagleburger. One misstep, one slip, one bad move and the consequences would be catastrophic. In his world there was no such a thing as a minor slip.

There are many common expressions that are, upon close examination, totally in error. One of those expressions is "Cash makes no enemies." In fact, cash does nothing but make enemies. The more cash you have, the more enemies you make. Relatives transubstantiate to leaches and in-laws to brigands. Everyone you have ever known believes in wealth by osmosis, that friendship entitles them to put their hand in your till. You are expected to donate at the Platinum level, place half-page advertisements at the full page rate and tip above 20%. If you buy a car out of town the local paper will snipe and if you buy a car in-town you will be accused of putting on airs. Dealmakers will sequester in your waiting room and investment counselors will haunt your dreams.

But Randolph had a solution: he had no cash. All the money was the bank's, he was just the servant of Mammon. It was a lie everyone knew was a lie but there was no cash to be had. All moneys from the bank were called loans and all loans came with consequences – and this was another of those common expressions that, upon close examination, is completely wrong. There are only consequences to loans if the bank so chooses or, in Anchorage, as Randolph so chose. When Randolph so chose it was Richards who did the dancing.

The great difficulty with dancing at the bank was that the rules were constantly changing. In the halcyon days before June of 1950, before the Trenton mob and the IRS, land titles had been like playing cards. They were pieces of paper that everyone accepted with a wink and a nod as having a value of $1. They were traded for favors, automobiles, poker game winnings and assorted debts and obligations. They were transferred in such a disjoined and untimely manner that no one knew for sure who owned what or when. The same piece of property might be registered in separate land title books months apart under a handful of different names with no definitive provenance. No one particularly cared because raw land had little value and even if a chunk of real estate suddenly had real value, it was the responsibility of the title insurance company to unravel the rat's nest of interlocking chains of ownership.

After June of 1950, the dance tune and steps changed. The wild and wooly days of land title as playing cards came to an end. Banking changed too. It got big and regulated. There were more people watching and all of them were very nasty individuals. Land exchanges were no longer the cake walk they had once been. It was now an Age of Rosin, rosin being the by-product of turpentine that ballet dancers used on their slippers to keep from slipping. The relationship of Richards and Randolph metamorphosed from one of paper-to-paper memos to code words spoken but never recorded. Land transfers now truly became a dance of death.

Richards, as a young man, had grown up in New York where he had specialized in bookkeeping and accounting for small banks. Unfortunately small banks did not survive the Depression; neither did a lot of large ones. He bounced through a number of jobs until he ended up working on the United States government's National Recovery Act consolidation of a potpourri of highways along the East Coast into what became designated as US-1, the highway between Fort Kent, Maine and Key West, Florida. He was stabled in a warehouse with scores of other bookkeepers and accountants on the federal payroll and his assignment was the refurbishing of the Lower Free Bridge over the Delaware River. This was the bridge between Trenton, New Jersey and Morrisville, Pennsylvania. It had previously been called the Lower Trenton Toll Supported Bridge – a typically bureaucratic title – until the United States government took over the bridge and removed the toll booths. Then the term "Free" was added to its title.

The bridge was more commonly known as the "Trenton Makes Bridge" because of a gigantic lighted slogan that was mounted on the bridge's spans. On one span were the words TRENTON MAKES and on the next THE WORLD TAKES. The slogan was to remind everyone crossing the Delaware River that Trenton, New Jersey was a manufacturing center and the world was coming to its door for its goods. In 1952, when Cordova Benson came to Anchorage, Richards had a completely different take on the slogan. He now read it as TRENTON TAKES and WHAT ANCHORAGE MAKES.

Richards was never privy to any of the discussions in Randolph's private office. His duty was to provide the cover for those machinations. He was a trusted employee of the bank for three reasons. First, he was devious when it came to moving money. Second, he was paid very well because he understood that if there were any negative repercussions – legal or physical – he would be the only one left on end of a very fragile limb with the bank denying any culpability. Third, he was a significant silent partner in many transactions and, as a widowed septuagenarian with three married sons who lived in three different states in the Lower 48, he was going to be able to leave them a tangible legacy, something most bookkeepers could never be able to do.

In the early years of the 1950s the land transfers were made more complicated because money had to be involved. A decade earlier the land transfers had been between pioneers who had every intention of holding onto the real estate for their children who also lived in Alaska. But with the influx of outsiders in the late 1940s and 1950s there were more and more land owners who intended to make their nut in the northland and live a retirement of ease in a land of Alaskan fantasy; where it never snowed and there were no mosquitoes. Now the beneficiaries of the land transfers needed a value that was universally recognized so a bank could use a plot of land in Anchorage as collateral for a coffee plantation in Kona which had no snow but, unfortunately, was replete with mosquitoes.

Richards had no problem solving this particular problem because all that was required was an establishment of land value with all moneys transferred swallowed by the transfer. It was still a dance just to a different tune with more spectators. The mechanism was the same as before 1950s, just with established values for the real estate instead of a $1 face value. Now, to pay a debt in land, the bank would buy and rebuy and rebuy the same piece of property until a set amount was reached. If Randolph owed John Smith $90,000, for instance, Randolph's bank would buy John Smith's home for its assessed value of $30,000. Then it would sell it back to him for $1. The transaction would occur two more times. Since a mortgage is a debt the payoff was not income so there was no income tax due. At the end of the day, whenever that was, John Smith would have $90,000 tax free plus the property. The frosting to this lucrative cake was that the transactions were quiet and often stretched over so long a period that the IRS would not be able to connect the dots – primarily because the average stint of an IRS agent in Anchorage was two years.

When it came to dealing with Trenton, the process was substantially more complicated.

First, there had to be some manner of payout that was washed when it came out of laundry. Second, there had to be anchor documents which would bear the scrutiny of not only the IRS but the FBI as well. While the IRS were bean-focused, the FBI had an entirely different view of the universe. That agency did not just look at records, they made their own recordings, followed suspects and had a nasty tendency to find things that were supposed to be buried forever.

Third, and most important, the transactions had to bear local scrutiny. The IRS and the FBI had rotating agents and small matters became squashed in the juggernaut of politics and landing of big fish. But by 1952 the number of players in the game had increased as did the danger of slippage. Two men from Trenton had settled into Anchorage who were not expected to rotate out. They were working with two old timers who knew what was what, as the expression went. One of those old timers was a convicted murderer from Wyoming who was muscle and was suspected of at least one murder uncomfortably close to Randolph. Here was a man you could not keep close to you but, at the same time, could not allow to stray too far from the game. He had to be trusted but could not be trusted. Worse on two accounts, he was no fool and he was close to the Trenton mob.

Richards had never met the Eagleburger. He knew who he was, of course. Everyone did. That was part of the mystique of being muscle. He did not have to make an appearance; just the mention of his name would make people sweat square nails. He was kept at arm's distance. Richards had never met the Jerzies either. They were also kept at arm's distance. Only one man ever made an appearance at the bank, Jack Jonstad, a crusty pioneer who never met with Randolph. He only met with Richards. Every third Thursday at noon and the two went over the Anchorage Downtown Retail Liquor Dealer's Syndicate account.

Until March of 1964.

Elizabeth Scarborough

F or those who appreciate official scientific definitions, Chaos Theory is the study of nonlinear dynamics in which seemingly random events are actually predictable from simple deterministic equations. A more earthy translation is "Sh&^ happens." Between the two is the colloquial: all things are connected and the flapping a butterfly's wings in the Himalayas will create monsoons in South America.

There was real world proof of this connection in Anchorage in October of 1957. The impetus came from as far as one could go from Alaska and still be on planet earth: Sicily. Between October 10 and 14, evil incarnate Lucky Luciano met with more than 30 Sicilian and American Mafia leaders to plan the most profitable enterprise ever undertaken by the underworld: the smuggling and distribution of mega-tons of heroin and cocaine into the United States.

It was an ambitious plan because it was so simple. The Sicilians would be responsible for the importation and distribution of the megatons of drugs in the United States and the American families would collect "franchise fees." The Sicilians liked the deal because they suddenly had an open market for their drugs. The Americans liked the deal because they got paid for doing nothing. Luciano liked the deal because he was a student of economics. The tremendous increase in the volume of heroin and cocaine was going to drive the price down making it afford-able to a whole new class of buyers: working class Americans, black and white.

It was an ambitious plan that succeeded. But there were unexpected consequences. While law enforcement officials were not privy to the discussions in Palermo, it did not take them long to understand what was going on. Even more important for the long run, several years earlier the people of the United States had been introduced to the term, concept and power of organized crime by the public hearings of the Kefauver Commission. For the first time the public became familiar with the names and faces of organized crime figures like Tony "Joe Batters" Accardo, Louis "Little New York" Campagna, Mickey Cohen, Frank Costello, Jake "Greasy Thumb" Guzik, Meyer Lansky, and Paul "The Waiter" Ricca. While the FBI under the control of J. Edgar Hoover failed to take organized crime seriously, the IRS did not make the same mistake. It went after organized crime figures where it hurt: their money. Across the United States generally and in New Jersey specifically, the IRS made it presence known. The agency went from broad brush to nitpicking and once the substance of the October 1957 meeting in Palermo became known, agency scrutiny became microscopic.

The new age came to Anchorage with a call from "Fat Louie" Grimaldi to a man known around Anchorage as Cordova Benson. Benson's real name was not generally known. He preferred it that way. To keep his identity secret and blend in with the lounge locals, he took his pseudonym by combing the names of an Alaskan city, Cordova, and a street, Benson. Everyone knew it was a phony but no one wanted to challenge a wise guy from Trenton who had Eagleburger as a bosom buddy and business partner.

But there was one person in Anchorage who did not give a hairy rat's ass about Benson, Eagleburger, Dorchester or

Jonstad: Elizabeth Scarborough. She didn't have to; she worked for the IRS.

That was the good news. The bad news, like tornados and spiders, came in pairs. She was an Alaskan and was going to be in the Anchorage office until Hell froze over or the Russians invaded. Neither was expected to happen in her lifetime. Then came the second pair: she was 30 years old in 1957 and had spent three years as a financial investigator for the United States Attorney in New York City, mob-investigation central. She took crap from no one – and that included Elton Randolph and Z. E. Eagleburger. She knew the former from cocktail parties and the latter from his continued appearances defending his wide range of businesses none of which had paperwork because of grease fires, flooding of Ship Creek, absent accountants, nefarious employees and sun flares. Both former and latter read her like a book because she told them, nose-to-nose, which book she was reading and on which page she was turned. The book from which she was reading was the United States Tax Code and she gave each of them a copy. Randolph gave his to Jerry Richards and that was the last time she talked with Randolph – even at cocktail parties.

The great strength of the IRS is that it wants money, not necessarily convictions. What this meant was that if you flipped early and completely, the agency was willing to cut you a deal. To the minions of organized crime before the death of Hoover in 1972, cooperating with the IRS did not get you in trouble with the FBI. The IRS would routinely pass along organized crime information to the FBI which did nothing and rarely passed along such documentation to local authorities. It soon became apparent to the mobsters that you were better off paying what the IRS said you owed than pushing your luck. If you popped above the radar and the local press got your name, there would be a hue and cry for an investigation which invariably lead to tragic consequences for the wise guys. So, when the IRS showed up, the wise guys played the game the agency's way.

But for the Jerzies, Anchorage was a real problem. While it was true that the money was being laundered and the paper trail clear, it was the root of the scheme that was causing headache. While the money was clean from its deposit in the bank through the land transactions, its legitimacy from the lounges to the bank was suspect. Before June of 1950, the lounges had made regular payments to the Anchorage Downtown Retail Liquor Dealer's Syndicate in a form called dues. Much of it was in cash and since the Syndicate kept good books, no one had to wonder where the money had come from or where it was going. By 1954, with the arrival of the Jerzies, the form called dues had substantially increased in price and passed through the Syndicate less a modest handling fee. The IRS was not interested in the amount of the handling fee. That was a legitimate cost of business. That the Syndicate fee was substantially higher than in other cities across the county was not a concern of the IRS either because the cost of doing business in Alaska was higher than in those in other cities. What was of concern to the IRS was the numerous other charges, fees and assessments which the lounges, taverns and brothels were paying and which were being writing off as *business expenses*. The IRS did not consider extortion a *business expense* and denied the write-offs and went after back taxes for seven years.

That was the nose of the camel under the tent.

Steven DeBarr

S teven DeBarr was a distinguished member of the 30 Club. Even more impressive, he was one of the few triple winners in the JCC – one of them a double banger!! Both honors were highly prized by the hodge-podge collection of newspaper journalist still writing during the devastation of the industry by the internet, and they – both journalists and honors – were proof that, like the tortoise, crocodile and Komodo dragon, there were surviving extinct species.

The 30 Club was a venerated establishment populated by former journalists rather than an active ones. In the days when paper was king, news stories sent to editors had footers like "Page 1 of 3" and "Page 2 of 3" at the bottom of the first two pages and – 30 – at the bottom of the last page indicating that this was the final page of the story. Single page stories had the notation as well. This was the way that editors knew that a sheet of paper from the story had not been lost in transit. This all changed when journalists stopped using typewriters and began using computers. The – 30 – was then superfluous. Some of the old reporters still used the footer but out of habit rather than as a means of communication. DeBarr was one of three journalists in Alaska who still used the footer – 30 – and the other two were *emeritus*.

The JCC was another old but venerable club though its membership was more fantasy than reality. It was the Journalist Cliché Club, a loose collection of old journalists who kept trying to slip clichés into their new stories. Editors, even the new, young ones, were keenly aware of the JCC in its various incarnations across the country and rudely excised any clichés which appeared in stories that crossed their desks. DeBarr had three which he had been able to slip in – two of which were, oddly, because they were appropriate and as such the editors at the time let them see print. One was a story about a waste disposal vehicle which had skidded off a slippery turn and spilled its load into a local creek. "Haste Makes Waste" was the header to the photo and DeBarr built on the cliché in the article.

The second cliché to slip by the same editor was because it was enclosed in a quote. In an article on the weather service there was a paragraph on rain making. A weatherman was explaining that clouds could be seeded with silver iodide and dry ice which, the weatherman was quoted as saying, "which means that every dark cloud has a silver lining and that silver lining is rain." It wasn't a smooth cliché but it was, nevertheless, a cliché that made it into print.

His *pièce de résistance* was a double-whammy. The senior editor had been out with an attack of appendicitis and the sports reporter had been away getting married in Hawaii. DeBarr was assigned to cover a high school baseball game, a sport of which he knew only two things: it had four bases and was played with a ball thus the name of the contest. He endured 11 innings of a 9 inning game and wrote a review of the contest by starting with a double cliché: "The gnarly hand of fate allowed the Bengals to snatch defeat from the jaws of victory. . ."

One of the blessings of journalism is that the past never fades to obscurity. For most newspaper readers, the daily newspaper is a retelling of what happened the day before. Then the newspaper and the stories were consigned to the trash heap of history or the bottom of the bird cage, whichever was more convenient. For most readers there is no past, only the future and every day of that future is bright and full of promise and peril. Readers rarely understand that the problems they will face in that future have been metastasizing in the past. Bankruptcies, divorces and the side effects of partisan legislation are, to paraphrase DeBarr, the gnarly hand of fate reaching from the past into the future.

DeBarr was a high quality journalist but not because of his writing style which, as one editor had admonished him, was "as flowery as plastic roses on a coffin lid" – and this was from the editor who had excised all but two of DeBarr clichés. DeBarr was a high quality journalist because he knew where to find fascinating stories. Almost all of the younger print journalists – the *print* adjective being a hoot because journalists no longer used ink – and none of the so-called investigative reporters at the television stations, knew how to find stories. They simply fleshed out stories from press releases or incidents from the police scanner. DeBarr was more ambitious. He checked the court filings, plumbed the arrest records, asked for incident reports from the airport and called long-time acquaintances who had their ears to the ground in their respected industries. He was a male Chatty Cathy and was as interested in rumor as he was in a hard news story.

One of his long term efforts was following obituaries. It wasn't so much that he was a ghoul as much as he was a news miner. What he did know and was willing to take advantage of was the Freedom of Information Act. Basically stated, when anyone dies all of their municipal, state and federal records become public property. What this meant to DeBarr was that when a pioneer died and there was a hint of impropriety, DeBarr would request the deceased's records from the FBI. The records cost nothing but took months to arrive. Nine times out of ten there was nothing worth reporting. But then there was that tenth time out of ten.

One dull afternoon at the press – and there were many of those – DeBarr got an email ("Curse you electronic media!" he thought) from an Arizona paper stating that a snowbird by the name of Vernon Samson – a winter resident of Phoenix and a summer resident of Anchorage –had died at the ripe age of 94. A widower, his son had turned over his father's papers to the local library which included an explosive autobiographical manuscript which included the names Jack Jonstad, A. R. Winston, Z. E. Eagleburger, Harold Drochester and Cordova Benson. Did any of these names mean anything to DeBarr?

Only one name did: A. R. "Ray" Winston. He had been the Chief of Police in the 1940s. DeBarr knew that because he had done a profile of the Anchorage Police Department. Winston had been so crooked he had been buried by screwing him into the ground. ("Bless you electronic media!" he thought) and emailed back that A. R. "Ray" Winston had been the Chief of Police in Anchorage and had left under a cloud. What else was in those papers that Samson's son had donated to the library and would the reporter please send him a copy of the obituary so he could go after Samson's FBI file?

Sandra Hamilton

Hamilton Construction, Inc. had been a fixture in Anchorage since the days of the Bering Sea Land Bridge. It was said, humorously at first, that when the first aboriginal had made it as far south as Anchorage, he laid for the foundation for the business and building both of which were still in existence in the 21st Century. Humor became reality when Hamilton Construction, Inc. was bought by a Native corporation. Then the catchphrase of the company's advertising was "In business in Anchorage since the dawn of time."

The progenitor of the company, Harold, had kept it alive in the pre-World War II era and watched the company boom beyond his wildest imagination with the Japanese invasion of Attu and Kiska. Overnight his mom-and-pop went to corporation and he was spending more time finding workers than raising walls. By the end of the war he was involved with the building of remote military sites from Dillingham to Barrow and out the Aleutians "until you ran into tomorrow." That was the expression used in those days because Attu, the last island, was six degrees into Eastern Hemisphere and, technically, on the other side of the then International Date Line.

Harold died shortly before the Berlin Airlift and the company passed to his wife and only son, George. Harold's wife did not live long after his death and by 1952 George and his wife,

Lucille, were the sole owners of a company that was bulging at every seam it had. It needed more skilled labor then could be found, more supplies than could be bought, more food than could be imported and more time than could be allocated. He had millions of dollars in construction contracts on his desk and no way to fulfill them – and the clock was ticking.

There is an old saying that the devil is easy to recognize. He comes to you late at night when you are very tired and makes you an offer you know you should refuse. Just after freeze-up in 1952, George Hamilton received a visit from a local union leader and a new man in town, Cordova Benson. The two had a rather interesting proposition. The pair was setting up a union affiliate which would hire highly qualified union men – as many as were needed – from the East Coast and send them to Alaska to work on the remote sites. The men – and a few women – would all be union people, of course, and their transportation to and from Alaska would be swallowed by the newly-forming union affiliate, the Anchorage Labor and Supply Cooperative. However – and this was such a large *however* that George saw coming before it arrived – the costs for such an enterprise were so large that it would be necessary for Hamilton Construction, Inc. to get all of its labor through the affiliate. Local workers would be given priority as long as they joined the union affiliate.

Benson went even further. With his contacts on the East Coast it would be possible to fully supply Hamilton Construction, Inc. with all of the building material it needed. The material could be ordered in bulk with other construction companies' orders, thus reducing its cost, and barged to arrive by break-up in 1953. The reason Benson could make such an offer was because he would be dealing with all of the Anchorage construction companies as a unit. If all of the construction companies agreed to order through his company, the volume of products would go up and, correspondingly, the price per piece would go down.

It was a very tempting offer and seven of the nine local construction companies felt they had no choice but to give it a try. The other two construction companies were both small and disreputable because one hired Natives and the other was being run into the ground by a dipso. Every operator felt that this offer was "too good to be true" and was fraught with great danger. But, on the other hand, every operator needed more men than the local workforce could provide and the workers coming in were hardly quality. Construction material was also in short supply in Alaska because of the building boom in the lower states. The G. I. Bill had made every veteran a home buyer and housing subdivisions were erupting from the soil of the lower states as fast as babies were being produced from the pairings of G.I. Joe with Rosie the Riveter. Business was business but a little cheating was expected so, to keep the *little cheating* to a minimum, the construction companies formed their own industrial organization to watch their collective back.

To say the relationship thus established was without difficultly would be in error. To say that the relationships was not profitable would also be in error. The 1950s were a decade of unbelievable growth for Anchorage and the moneys that the construction companies spent on labor and material were dwarfed by their profits. It was said that all you had to have to make money in Anchorage in the 1950s was a cash register.

But that was the 1950s. By 1962 the country was suffering from construction exhaustion. It was end of the Age of Eisenhower with its interstate highway, Levittowns and fat, white men in dull grey business suits running the country. Elvis Presley was rocking, American cars were rolling on 35 cent a gallon gasoline, Martin Luther King, Jr. was walking and in Anchorage, Sandra Hamilton was the CEO of Hamilton Construction, Inc. and President of the Anchorage Construction Company Alliance, the ACCA. Hamilton, in this case Sandra, had grown up in the construction industry and been educated at UC Berkeley.

She had not been part of any particular social movement of the day, but neither had she been inoculated against them. Rather, from her perspective as an economics major, she understood what Karl Marx never realized. The world did not move forward based on wages paid; it flowered by wages spent. A good economy depended on money spent in the marketplace, not how much people were making.

She was particularly sensitive to this missed lesson of Karl Marx because he had lived in a world that was shoulder-to-shoulder workers of the world from the Atlantic coast of France to the Caucasus. This meant that the term "local" had no real meaning when it came to labor. Being from Alaska she knew exactly what "local" meant. It meant Alaskan. Alaska was unlike any other place in America because it was so isolated. Anyone looking for a job in Berkeley had the entire Bay Area at his or her disposal. Someone looking for a job in Anchorage could only look in Anchorage. Every place else was far away. Far away meant transportation costs.

On the other hand – and she cringed at that economic cliché – a contained area like Anchorage forced money to circulate. Wages paid to local workers were spent in local shoe stores, local restaurants, local taverns, local theaters and local housing. Dollars did not leave town, they rolled through the city until they ended up in a bank where they were borrowed and thus began another cycle of fiscal perambulation. America's economic blessing was Anchorage's curse: the depth and spread of economic diversity in the lower states gave the economy strength. In Anchorage money was like blood; if too much left it died.

On January 1, 1962, Sandra Hamilton told the ACCA that Hamilton Construction, Inc. was no longer going to be honoring the contract with the decade-old Anchorage Labor and Supply Cooperative that had been supplying manpower and construction materials. The salad days of DEW, NORAD, LORAN and WHITE ALICE were gone and unlikely to come again. Construction had gone from boom to bust and the transportation costs of flying part-time workers into Anchorage were not worth the moneys paid. While Hamilton Construction, Inc. was going to continue to have a union shop, the company was not going to be buying any more construction material exclusively from the union affiliate. There was plenty of such material available on the open market and she wanted the Law of Competition to drive down prices and raise quality.

There was not a single person on the Executive Council of the ACCA who did not feel exactly the same way as Sandra Hamilton. She was hardly the youngest person on the Executive Council but she was the only one to openly challenge what every other member feared. What they all knew to be true was that the union-affiliated company in question was linked with Jerzies and though there were only two in town, the two had connections which could make business difficult. The subsidiaries of the multi-state construction companies on the Council had suffered dyspeptic consequences when it came dealing with the ilk of Jerzies. Shipments were lost, property destroyed, workers frightened off the job and other such inconveniences. Further, it seemed that their kind was more a virus than an infection. One could find an antidote for an infection but you had to outlive a virus.

But she had two good points. First, not matter how it was sugarcoated, the Anchorage Labor and Supply Cooperative was run out of Trenton and that's where they money was going. Those dollars were not going into the local economy. A decade earlier the industry may have needed a company like the Cooperative but not now. It was time for a change.

Second, one only had read the national newspaper to see which way the wind was blowing. John F. Kennedy was in the White House and his brother Robert had a hard-on for organized crime. The writing was on the wall and the ACCA had better not be found hand-in-glove with Trenton when the long arm of Attorney General of the United States reached Anchorage.

There was third reason which was not stated but everyone knew. Hamilton was married to a local construction union president. There was not a single person in the room – or a married one – who did not doubt that she had discussed this move with her husband. There was also not a person in the room who doubted that the unions were in favor of this move. It was as much in the Anchorage unions' interests to eliminate the Anchorage Labor and Supply Cooperative from the local scene as it was for the ACCA. In this both labor and management were in agreement – and Sandra Hamilton had no problem delivering the news personally.

Harry Scarborough

Everybody on the lounge strip knew Harry the Barber. Not that many knew him as Harry Scarborough. To everyone he was Harry the Barber, the colored man who cut your hair, shined your shoes, told great stories and didn't know who you were if he met you uptown. He talked like he came from North Carolina which, in fact, he had. But he was unlike blacks in North Carolina.

Harry had come north before the war and ended up in the 370th Regimental Combat Team, the first blacks to be in a combat unit since the First World War. The unit landed in Sicily and fought their way north bloody step by bloody step under the command of "Old Blood and Guts" George Patton. Patton didn't care what color his troops were as long as they could fight, would fight and that they did fight.

After the fall of Rome, Harry was transferred to France where he witnessed the liberation of Paris in August of 1944. He mustered out in 1945 and went to New York where he learned to be a barber on the G.I. Bill. Then he bounced his way across America with a ratty suitcase and a pocket full of scissors and combs and ended up in Anchorage in 1955, as far as you could go in the United States from North Carolina and still speak English.

Harry was hardly what you would expect of a seasoned combat veteran. He was only about 5' 2, bulky rather than slim, had delicate hands and massive feet. He wore bunny boots year round and usually military issue trousers. At least that was what he wore at work and that was when most people saw him. He roomed at the Crystal Bathhouse and over the years lived with or was associated with a number of the working girls in the brothel, some of them blacker than he was.

He was in the perfect city for a barber with military experience in 1955. The Alaskan economy was exploding and the military bases, two of them, were doubling in size. Most of his clients were military personnel who required a specific kind of cut. Harry knew that cut and men were standing in line for the $2 buzz. They were standing line because he was in the perfect location for a military-style barber shop. He had a one-man stand, more of a crib than a shop, on Fourth Avenue between B and C. He was on the south side of the street, sandwiched between a hamburger joint and a lounge that had been going out of business in the same location for ten years. Enlisted men and noncoms would grow their hair as long as possible until ordered to get a haircut. Then they would follow orders by going down to the lounge strip, carouse for a handful of hours and just before heading back to Elmendorf or Fort Richardson – and with their last $2 – sit for a 15-minute military haircut. For another dollar Harry would shine your boots but you had to drop them off the night before. Everyone loved his shines because they passed muster on base and were so good that every pair of boots in which you could see yourself was known as a Harry Shine – which, to Southerners, was a pun. To Northerners it was just a stupid reference to a black man.

Harry knew everyone on the strip and everything that was going on. He knew all of the good brothels, the best women, the worst gambling dens and where you could get moonshine if that's what you wanted. He was most loved by the Anchorage

Police Department. While he was a long-term, bonafide member of the DKN Club, "Don't Know Nothing," he was also the perfect backchannel to anyone anywhere on the lounge strip. If the police needed to talk with someone, all they had to do was stop by Harry's shop and mention it. Harry would always say the same thing, that the name was familiar but it was "on the far side of yesterday" and if he remembered from where he knew the name he'd let them know. The police would then say they were going next door for a burger and, like clockwork, about half an hour later whomever it was they were looking for would magically show up in the same burger stand. Harry, of course, knew absolutely nothing about how that particular person had gotten the message to show up to talk to the police.

Had Eagleburger still been in town when Harry set up his chair he would have loved the service Harry provided. It kept the police out of the lounge strip establishments and satisfied every excuse they had for entering on official business. Most of the policemen were married so there was not a lot of slumming and even if they went drinking the cops were all so well-known that they could not go undercover. So they did neither; they let Harry be their eyes and ears even though he was a bonafide member of the DKN Club.

Harry was welcome uptown for a number of reasons, the biggest one being his membership in DKN Club. He was a regular member of the Anchorage Unreformed Methodist Church – the term "unreformed" was on the plaque over the door because the minister was firm in his belief that the "reformed" were on the road to Hell. Harry never said he knew the difference between a "reformed" and "unreformed" Methodist and most likely did not care. He was a man of God on every day of the week. He clearly understood the frailty of the human spirit and had more than a few sins to repent for, most of them having been committed in a war zone but were sins nonetheless. Just as important, he and his woman of the moment – and there were not that many over the years – were pious in their devotion. It was not as if they, the women, were intent on washing away the sins they were committing during the week. It was because the Holy Spirit was in all of us and God, in His righteousness, recognizes good people caught in bad situations.

Harry, for his part, was blind to the moral transgressions of the uptown people he met downtown. He knew the uptown people who were going to the gambling dens, brothels and lounges of Fourth Avenue by name, reputation and unique moral weakness. But he did not recognize a single one of them north of Sixth Avenue.

There was one exception to this rule: Josiah Fitzsimmons. Fitzsimmons was the pastor of the Anchorage Unreformed Methodist Church who, oddly, also came from North Carolina. Fitzsimons was on a mission but it was not to expiate any sin or sins he knew he had. Neither was it to expiate any sin he had originally acquired by being human. His mission was to pull individuals from the pit of sin, one at a time if necessary. No one was without sin and he knew such was the natural state of man. Be it Chapel Hill, Robeson County, Campobasso where a German bullet pierced his helmet but not his skull or Montecassino where the allies had wiped a 1,500 year old monastery and library off the face of the earth because someone thought the Germans might be hiding tanks in the rectory, Fitzsimmons recognized that he could not change 100,000 years of human behavior. All he could do was find and save one person at a time. Anchorage was just as good a place as any to fulfill his mission.

Like Harry, Fitzsimons had come to Alaska to get as far away from North Carolina as possible. He still had a wife in the Tar Heel State where she was looking after a father sinking into Alzheimer's. This did not free him from any marital obligations but it did increase the amount of time he could spend saving souls. His particular mission was young girls, too young to know that life in the brothels was a dead end profession. These young women were primarily black with a sprinkling of Native girls from the villages. When Fitzsimons learned of a girl who was too young to be in a brothel, he would extricate the child and place her with a good family in Anchorage. His track record was hardly sterling, about one success for every six or seven extractions every six months. But as far as Fitzsimmons was concerned, not every individual could be saved and one every six months was better than none at all.

For his part Harry kept Fitzsimmons informed as to which brothel had underage prostitutes. Harry, however, was not simply playing second fiddle to a savior. He was working with the full cooperation of the brothels because women under the age of 18 were very bad for business. They had parents in Ohio and Indiana who contacted the local police who sent inquiries that the Anchorage Police Department could not ignore. Native villages reported runaways to the Alaska State Troopers who were, quite literally, the kiss of death to the lounge strip and brothels. This was because the Troopers were unaware of the unique relationship between the Anchorage Police and the businesses of the lounge strip.

Or they didn't care.

If the State Troopers got a missive from one of their own in a remote village, they went looking for the runaway teenager. Flights to Anchorage were frequent but most of the girls never made it any further south. Anchorage only had 6,000 residents and two dozen brothels so it was not hard to trace the runaway if she were Native. So the Troopers would go brothel to brothel and did not care who was inconvenienced – landlord or john. Once the runaway was found there were legal consequences for the brothel and that was when the lawyer bills started to mount.

To keep peace in the lounge-police family, so to speak, it was most desirable for everyone for someone – name and face unknown on the lounge strip and in the brothels – to simply extricate the young woman. Then the matter could be handled uptown by the Anchorage Police, out of town by the Alaska Troopers or out of the Territory (later the state) by the minions of law and order in whatever jurisdiction was affected. This arrangement left everyone in Anchorage happy and no one out on a limb.

While this arrangement worked very well north of Sixth Avenue, there was a rather substantial fly in the ointment. Not all brothels were north of Sixth Avenue and those to the south of Sixth Avenue were not privy to the unique arrangement of the lounge strip. These were freelance operations, most of them scattered in the hinterlands. Several specialized in young women and one in very young individuals, male and female. Most of the slummers knew of these establishments and avoided them because they were, as the expressions went, "bad news just waiting to happen."

That "bad news" came with a bang in an unrecorded July of early 1960s. On a Tuesday which forever became known among the lounge lizards as "Blue Ticket Tuesday," or more commonly as BTT. The Anchorage Police knew of the existence of about a half-dozen of these establishments but there was nothing they could do about them for the simple reason that the brothels were not within the city limits. The Alaska State Troopers knew of the existence of these houses but could not do anything about them because there had been no complaints so they had no legal reason to raid the houses. The FBI knew of the houses but had more important cases to investigate. The people who were most upset were, oddly, the Jerzies when they discovered that their man in Anchorage, Cordova Benson, had been freelancing by going into business on his own and thus in competition with the downtown Jerzie brothels.

The festering problem had grown to the point that something had to be done and soon. Too many incidents had made it into the *Anchorage Times* and the disgust level of those who did know of the function of those establishments had reached a breaking point. But there was a rather odious collection of problems with shutting these establishments down. First, some of the patrons of those establishments were highly respected members of the community. Even if the landlords could be taken to court, the subsequent trials would sully many important names. Further, no one knew how knowledgeable the Trenton family was as to what was happening on property they may have or may not have owned. While Eagleburger was gone by this time, there was always the fear that the Jerzies could upset the apple cart of the arrangement by having muscle flown in from the East Coast. What was needed was a surgical strike that could close the brothels in question, place the underage boys and girls under legal care, punish the landlords, send a message to the Jerzies that such houses were beyond the limits of the understood relationship and, at the same time, do all of this quickly, quietly and solve the problem permanently.

The solution was as clear as a boulder in a teacup.

It just took a little tap dancing.

It would take years for the story to leak out which, for those involved, was exactly what had been intended. What basically transpired was that at 11 p.m. on a Monday night that has been lost to history – along with the Special Anchorage Assembly Meeting Minutes of that five minutes of Anchorage history (if such Minutes were ever taken) – a special meeting of the Anchorage Assembly extended the city limits *as far south as but just north of* the legal claim of the Crow Creek Mine in what is now Girdwood. This gave the Anchorage Police the legal right to raid the establishments.

For the six hours that the city limits of Anchorage had been extended, midnight to 6 a.m.

It has been suggested that Harry the Barber apparently knew of the impending raids because not a single owner of any of the lounge strip establishments was in Anchorage that evening or the next morning. The Reverend Fitzsimmons was, he alleged in later years when the BTT became part of the underground history of the Northland, "taken by surprise" when he was presented with a collection of 13 young boys and girls who had been rescued from brothels of which he knew nothing.

But these activities were only a miniscule part of the solving the problem. There was still the issue of how to keep the establishments closed permanently, maintain the propriety of their records and thereafter make certain that Benson and Jonstad and/or the Jerzies did not repeat the error of the past. This was quite a collection of chores but in Alaska in an unrecorded July of the 1960s all things were possible.

From the dim memories of the old timers it appeared that, strangely, as the six bawdy houses were raided in unison, all of the paperwork from the buildings suffered from spontaneous combustion. This was the scientific term for consumable items which, contrary to the laws of science, suddenly explode into fire on their own and are completely consumed. All suspected underage boys and girls were escorted to the Anchorage Unreformed Methodist Church. The names of such individuals were not recorded because the city does not release records of alleged those who were under the age of 18 at the time of the incident. Those owners and residents of the establishment 18 years or older were, for their own safety, escorted to the Anchorage Airport where they were placed – again for their own safety – aboard a waiting, long-range aircraft which may or may not have been a military airplane piloted by the most close-mouthed pilot in Alaska, George "Gypsy" Davis. The aircraft used has never been identified and the United States Air Force has no record that any of its passenger planes were aloft on that night.

Further, according to local legend, onto that plane went about 10 brothel entrepreneurs along with Cordova Benson and Jack Jonstad. It is rumored that somehow the Trenton family had been informed of the happenings via one of their own in Alaska who kept a low profile for the simple reason that the Trenton family was not willing to trust one of its own to operate any-where without supervision. The plane left at approximately 1 a.m. and, according to "Gypsy," the plane left Alaskan airspace "some time before 6 a.m." when the temporary extension of the boundaries of the City of Anchorage reverted back to their old monument markers. At that moment the matter of the fate of the passengers was no longer a City of Anchorage or State of Alaska matter.

It is alleged though no one knows for a fact, that upon landing in Seattle there was a phone call waiting for Cordova Benson. The conversation, again allegedly, was short and one-sided. Shortly thereafter Benson and Jonstad returned to Anchorage. Thereafter there were no more illicit brothels funded with Jerzie moneys.

By the time the story of BTT broke into public knowledge late in 2010, only Harry the Barber was still alive and reachable. He was still living in Anchorage, 95 years of age, volunteering at the Anchorage Unreformed Methodist Church, the father of six children and sixteen grandchildren, none of whom was in an illegal enterprise. When asked of the BTT by historians from the Alaska Historical Publication Association, all Harry said was "well, that's on the far side of yesterday."

Beatson "Jingo" Jefferson

" First off I'd like to thank the Alaska Historical Publication Association for making this conference possible. As you all know, since most of you are history teachers, getting students let alone the general public to appreciate history is like pulling teeth. As far as they are concerned, history is the most boring subject at school and is basically stories told by old war horses like me. To a certain extent that's true. But it's only boring because that's the way the school district wants the subject taught – the Pilgrims by Thanksgiving and the Civil War by Christmas – and the only thing war horses like me are good for are stories of the good old days which, if you lived them, in many cases, weren't all that good.

For those who have never heard of me, and that should be most of you, I'm Beatson "Jingo" Jefferson. Sergeant Jefferson for about 24 years, from 1941 to 1965. I picked up the name "Jingo" because I used to swear a lot when I was young and one of my officers was a Baptist who did not want anyone taking the name of the Lord in vain. So he got me to saying Jingo instead of Jesus H. Christ and ever since it's been my nickname. My first name is for the Beatson Mine on La Touche Island where my father was working when I was born.

I was born in Cordova so long ago that weren't making calendars yet. My parents were working for the Beatson Mine on La

Touche Island and they hadn't built the hospital on the island so my mother took the ferry to Cordova and I was born in what was then the general hospital. I was raised on La Touche until the price of copper went to five cents a pound and the mine closed. My parents chose to go to the new city of Anchorage where my dad got a job on the Alaska Railroad and my mother worked odd jobs around town including being a waitress at the Oyster Loaf. That was the all night restaurant which used to be across the street from the old courthouse and across the street from the log cabin that is now the Visitor Center. Many of you probably remember it as the lunch counter of Woolworth's.

I could not wait to get out of Anchorage and as soon as I graduated from high school I joined the Army. I was sent to Fort Ord, which was just as wet and cold as La Touche Island, and when the war started, I was sent to Pearl Harbor. For the first year of the war all I did was clean up the island and build bunkers. Then I was sent – guess where? – back to Alaska because the Japanese had taken Attu and Kiska. Back in those days the Army actually read your personnel file and it wanted to have Alaskan boys on the ground up here. So back I came to Anchorage and I was stationed at Fort Richardson; there wasn't an Elmendorf Air Force Base yet.

When I got here in January of 1943 Anchorage was booming. There were buildings exploding out of every vacant lot, military vehicles were parked on the sidewalk, you were sleeping three and four to hotel rooms and it took you a 15, 20 minutes to walk a few blocks on the sidewalk. I lived on Fort Richardson and we trained for combat in the Aleutians. We ate in the snow, slept in the rain, marched with wet boots and dug into the muskeg with those god-awful adjustable shovels. We were going to be the invasion force to finally drive the Japanese off the island and out to sea.

We trained hard, day and night, snow and rain, and I have to tell you that every one of us was scared, scared, scared. We had heard what had happened on Attu and we were expecting the Battle of Kiska to be worse. When we hit the beaches we fully expected to be racked with machine gun fire. I knew I was not going to make it back alive so I had put all of my personal belongings in a box and slid it under the bed in my parents' room. I didn't tell them it was there. They found it by accident after I got back from Kiska and we had a good laugh.

Well, the joke was on us. As most of you know there wasn't a Japanese soldier to be found on Kiska. After the Battle of Attu the Japanese figured they were not going to be able to hold the islands – why they wanted them in the first place is still a mystery to me – and they skedaddled home.

For the next two years I bounced around the South Pacific but I didn't see that much action. I wanted to see action, volunteered for action but was never chosen. I guess I should thank my lucky stars because a lot of men, boys really, never came back. My big moment was to be the invasion of Japan and I sitting on a ship in an armada that stretched as far as the eye could see off the Japanese coast when we heard that the Japanese had surrendered. All we know was that some kind of a bomb had gone off and that had ended the war. That was as close as I got to the fighting.

By the time the war ended I was a sergeant and I did not want to leave the Army. I did not have any skills I could use in the real world – that's what we called it then, the 'real world' – and, frankly, thought I was too old to learn a trade. I was 20 and knew *everything* – just like your grandkids!

I wanted to go to Europe but when I put in my papers I got shunted to Alaska. Back to Alaska. Why? Because the Army said I was needed there. There was a massive build-up of military might and the Army needed experienced soldiers just in case the Russians invaded.

The Russians invaded?

Where the heck did that idea come from?

I was told to shut and go.

So I went.

If I thought Anchorage had been crazy when I was here in 1942, five years later it was bedlam. The town had doubled in size, possibly tripled and there was every kind of contractor in the world here. Everyone was making money including the PFCs. They'd do a shift on Fort Richardson and bounce in the lounges for another eight hours for twice what they were making on base. Every GI from sergeant on down was working off duty hours downtown and making, like I said, more than Uncle Sam was paying.

As you can see I am a big man so I had no trouble getting a job as a bouncer. It was also easier for me because I had grown up in Anchorage so I knew all of the lounge operators. Even better, they knew me and my parents so I got the good jobs. I met a lot of the pioneers then, men and women who are long gone now, the ones who actually made Anchorage. I was too young to see the seedy side of the business so to me guys like Zabriskie, Silvestri, Jonstad, Drochester, Fortunato and Eagleburger were legends in their own time. Those years were golden for me, my age of innocence.

When Anchorage broke into the 1950s I got a new job, one that I didn't even know existed in the Army. It probably didn't but it was needed. There were so many military personnel and their families downtown that the Army needed people on the ground to take care of military personnel problems. This was just a nice way of saying that they needed men who would be MPs but not upset the local business people. I got booted to sergeant and assigned to keep the peace in downtown Anchorage. I was about 26 and put in charge of five men, the oldest being, maybe 19. Our job was to walk the streets and break up fights and such that involved military personnel. No officers or noncoms, just the lower ranks. That was fine with me because it was basically a graveyard shift which meant I could bounce during the day and then walk the lounge strip at night. I was living at home so I didn't have to take the bus out the base like my men did.

It did not take me very long to get to know all of the downtown movers and shakers at the time. Everyone knew I was with the military because they saw me in a uniform all night and in civvies during the day. The old timers knew me as one of their own, a local, so they would tell me things and include me in conversations. Remember, I was still pretty young but boy was I proud to be included in the conversations – especially when I was told to tell no one what was being talked about.

Perhaps the truest thing I can see about Anchorage in those years was that we were a real community then, something we are not now. The uptown and downtown movers and shakers knew each other, drank with each other, gambled with each other and covered each other's back. Publically they may have been enemies but that ended at 5 p.m. and everyone drank together. As an example, I remember the *Anchorage Times* slamming the Alaska Railroad for something. I can't remember what it was but it was day after day of anti-Railroad editorials. Right in the middle of the campaign something happened to the newsprint press. It broke and they could not get the paper out until it got fixed. So the editor of the newspaper went down to the Alaska Railroad mechanical shop and got the press fixed. I think the Railroad people had to work on it all night. No charge. Every one of those mechanics knew that the *Anchorage Times* was attacking their boss, their source of income. But that didn't matter. This was Anchorage and when someone from Anchorage needed help, everyone was there.

That's exactly the way the military was in those days too. No one ever told the Commander what was being done in the name of the military, it was just done. You didn't fill out any paperwork, you just did it. It could be using a Jeep to take someone to the hospital or giving cases of C rations to the city for the homeless. You didn't ask permission, you just did it. The military didn't care. The command structure wanted good relations with the locals so they turned a blind eye to a lot of transgressions.

There was also another reason the military had a blind spot for local activities. It's hard to get Alaskans to understand now but we were on the front lines of the Cold War. No one was shooting at us but the military command expected it to happen at any time. We were building Cold War bases across Alaska as fast as we could and recruiting secret agent types to stay behind just in case the Russians invaded.

They were also worried that there were spies in Alaska. While this is a wild idea today, it wasn't so farfetched then. There have always been a lot of foreigners in Alaska – in America too – and we had just gone through four years of war with the Russians as our allies. They had been in Fairbanks in a very big way with Lend-Lease and after the war some of the Russians had come back, married local girls and found jobs in Alaska. Some of them were working construction on these supposedly secret military bases that everyone knew about. They were cooks and janitors and bartenders and taxi cab drivers – just like today. Russians have played a big part in Alaska history. We were owned by Russia until 1869 and a lot of the Russian trappers married Native women. The last Territorial governor, Mike Stepovich, was of Russian extraction. So was Zabriskie. It would not have been hard for the Russians to have slipped some spies into Anchorage. The only way the military was going to catch those spies was for the locals to report them.

The military also did not want was any trouble downtown because that was where the barges came in with the supplies for all of those bases. They didn't want any strikes. They didn't want any shut downs. You can understand that. The way you keep things humming along is to show the locals that you are a good guy. You bend over backwards for them. This meant giving a lot of support to the local groups. Sometimes it meant flying Santa Claus around to the villages and the Coast Guard was well-known for arriving in small coastal villages, cleaning them up, painting the church, repairing the dock, things like that. The Coast Guard still does it. It's a way of keeping the locals happy and that pays dividends in the long run.

In those heady days of the 1950s up to the Earthquake I saw a lot of military support that was, as you would say today, "off the books." Things just happened. If a credible person needed something, he just asked. Most of the time the military didn't ask any questions. Most of the time they didn't want to. I remember one time there was riot – and I mean a **riot** – at one of the canneries. I don't remember what the problem was but it boiled over big time. We are talking about a dozen people, men and women, running wild, shooting at each other, destroying equipment, and burning some out-buildings. There were too many rioters for the local police, all one of him, and there were no State Troopers then. The first I knew about it was when a six-pack showed up in downtown Anchorage and shoved me and my crew inside. We were plopped down in a C-130 and given batons. Three hours later we were chasing rioters through a cannery and collecting them one at a time. When we had all 14 or 15 of them, we packed them into the C-130 and flew them to Elmendorf and then on to Seattle. Then we turned them over to the United States Marshal.

Keep in mind that the cannery was not a military establishment. It was a private company. You could never do that today. But this was Alaska in the 1950s. The military looked at itself as an arm of the community and we really needed that. Like when the Earthquake came we needed manpower and building material right away. The bases provided both and flew in critical supplies – medicine, hospital equipment. We didn't really need a field hospital but if we had the military would have provided it.

Which leads me to comment on something that is missing in today's military. That's the looseness of the chain of command. Lamentably, I must add. In the United States Army I served in there was not only a respect of the individual but a willingness to let your men handle the problem. The general attitude was that the men – and women because there were quite a few serving during the Second World War – serving under you were to be given as free a hand as possible. Officers did not get involved in the small stuff. Or, in many cases, big stuff. Officers depended on their men and women to do the right thing and did not interfere. You won't see that happening today. Today the chain of command today is really a chain. The message coming down from the top is one of micromanagement, "Don't do anything, let me make the decision. Let me make every decision." That means that every action has to run up the chain for approval. When the decision comes back down it is changed, altered and most of the time unworkable. The best person to solve a problem is the person with the problem.

A lot of what happened for the better in those post World War II days in Anchorage could never happen today because the command structure is so rigid that no one wants to make a decision. So a lot of things that could be done, should be done, ought to be done, never get done because no one wants to take a chance or does not want to look bad if the action goes wrong – or worse, if the action goes right.

That's one of the main reasons I got out of the military. By 1972, the military I was in was not the military I had joined in 1941. The America of today is not the same as it was in 1940s, Alaskans are not the same as they were in the 1950s and Anchorage is a lot different today that it was in the 1960s. Change is not always good.

Over the past week, I've been reading the extracts of Vernon Samson's work in the local paper. I never knew Samson. I knew who he was but I never knew him personally. A lot of what he wrote about happened uptown and I didn't spend a lot of time there. But what he said about downtown was pretty much on the mark. I knew the people he wrote about but knew them when they were adults and I was in my 20s. A lot of the activities he wrote about were pretty much standard for the time. I was a small part of some of those events and forgotten all about them. The letters to the editors about how crooked the early day seemed to have been are the same people who think that life in hunky-dory because they've had the same good job most of their life and live uptown. Anchorage was a frontier boomtown in the 1950s and a lot of things happen in a boomtown that never make the papers. But legends are made in boomtowns and I thank God that I was in the right place at the right time to see some of those legends in the flesh – and take part in some of the events that the paper is revealing.

I'm looking forward to tomorrow's paper!

If you have any questions I'll do the best that I can to answer them."

Damien Oliver II

"I wish I could tell you more but frankly, looking over the documents you already have, there's not a lot more I can add. I'm here to cooperate, sure, but I can only tell you, will only tell you, what I know to be true. The early days are kind of hazy but you really don't care that much about those days, right? You just want to know what happened over the last four or five years, the time right before and right after the Earthquake. That time period I can remember pretty well.

Like a lot of the old timers I got into the lounge business during the war. We were too old to be drafted and too young to die and we had to do something. Before the war my daddy had what you'd call a hamburger joint down on Fourth Avenue and we made just enough money to live poorly as long as I washed the dishes and mom kept the books. That all changed with the war and we suddenly had people standing in line for burgers and dogs. The Japs had taken the last islands of the Aleutians and we had military coming in by the planeload. Then they, the military that is, started building the remote sites and things went from wild to crazy to out-and-out insane. We were making so much money so fast we took out the cash register and just dug change out of wood box behind the counter.

It didn't take dad long to see that the real money was in liquor so he squished the hamburger grill against the wall, ripped out the freezer and extended the joint back about 15 feet. That still wasn't enough room so we created a bar with the clothing store next door. Within a year we had to tear out the back walls of what had been both businesses and extended into a Quonset out back. Even then we still couldn't keep up with the business.

That's when the Anchorage Downtown Liquor Dealer's Syndicate came into being. We had a number of real pressing problems. We had too many customers and not enough liquor. No matter how much liquor came in we were running out. So we formed the Syndicate to start buying in bulk so the price would go down and the volume of liquor would go up. That worked like a charm because we, that is, the lounge owners, were buying liquor by the barge load – and the barges were coming once every ten days. It upset the airline companies because they'd been bringing in the liquor before but they charged an arm and a leg.

That's right. During the winter the liquor came in by truck. It was more expensive then but we didn't care. We just raised the price of the drinks. Everyone did.

The next problem – actually it wasn't like it was the next problem because it was happening at the same time – was dealing with the police. It started with the police chief then, Winston. He was a real hard time Charlie. I mean, here was a man who set up a hit of one of his own! That's the kind of a guy he was. He was triple A dangerous. And he was the head of the police department. When he came around we had to listen.

For the rest of the police force, they were OK guys. Underpaid and young but not bad in the New York sense of the term. They were also never crooked in the New York sense of the term either. But they had a bad job. Some Susie bluenose uptown would complain and pretty soon there'd be raid, a couple of people would get arrested and then things would just settle back down.

The lounge strip was an ongoing problem for the police because we had so many rowdies. Until the end of the war we had some donnybrooks with military guys fighting construction guys and military police and the Anchorage police trying to break everything up and everyone getting a black eye or a bloody nose. It was a fight an hour somewhere on the lounge strip and then there were the problems in the brothels which stretched from Fourth Avenue to about Sixth and back toward the cemetery.

But those weren't the real reason we formed the Syndicate. We were the downtown dealers and we had to make sure everyone knew we were the Fourth Avenue lounge owners. We were the ones with the problems. The other businesses that sold liquor from, say, Sixth Avenue south, called themselves midtown businesses. They felt they were sophisticated and didn't want to associate with the scum of the earth on the lounge strip. They sold a higher class liquor which had to come in by plane. Uptown folks drank there unless they went slumming along Fourth Avenue.

The problems we had in the early days was normal stuff like water and sewer, storm drains, trash and taxi cab double parking. Hell, the strip had been built when Anchorage had maybe 3,500 people and we were seeing that many *a month* coming and going. There were lots of problems. That's why we formed the Syndicate. None of us individually had time to fight the sewer and water utility and city hall and the work on the storm drain problem and the taxi cab problem and on and on and on. That was the job of the Syndicate and, frankly, the problems were so large that no group could solve them. It just wasn't possible.

Making matters worse along the lounge strip there were some really bad eggs in the business. I'm talking about people who killed people. Organized crimes is not the term I want to use but let's just say that there were about a dozen very bad people in the lounge business and you did not cross them. You only got into a fight in their establishment once.

But that all changed in the early 1950s and I see from your documents that you already know that. Three or four things happened at the same time. The police chief was honest and expected the cops to be the same. But they were overwhelmed. Unless there was something really bad happening, there wasn't much they did on the lounge strip. We were left to solve our own problems so we did. Every lounge had a bouncer but that was it. We were overwhelmed. None of us were heavy-weights and we were seeing at least a fight a night per lounge and more often it was a brawl. There was only one guy we could call if we really had to: Harold Drochester. But you already know about him. If we really needed some muscle we called him. He didn't work for the Syndicate but he'd take care of matters as a personal favor. We paid him for his services but his wasn't a regular gig. When we knew we were going to need him, we made a call.

Then you guys showed up. Until about 1950 or 1951 there were really no business rules. You opened up a lounge and that was that. You sold drinks and food and there wasn't anyone looking over your shoulder. Prices were the same all over town. Food cost the same all over town. No one charged more than anyone else 'cause we were all in the same boat, so to speak. There was a lot of gambling and every once in a while someone would get raided but it was no big deal. There was a fine that was usually paid quickly and that was that. Every once in a while a brothel could get closed but that was only if someone created a problem up town, some blue nose, you know. But other than that we were pretty much left alone on the lounge strip.

After you feds showed up everyone had to keep books. That made it hard 'cause a lot of the money we made had been under the table, mostly gambling, brothels and some drugs. Suddenly we had to deal with the IRS and the FBI in a big way. They weren't just federal agencies in the Lower 48 anymore; they were right here in town and they were aggressive like the police had never been.

We, the Syndicate that is, were up to our ears in problems. Not a single problem from the war had been solved and the number of customers kept going up. We were using outhouses because the toilets were plugging, water tasted like sulfur and we had to buy generators because the power in the lounges kept going off. We were now seeing *more* than a fight a night in the lounges and the police weren't doing anything. We had tried to clean up the industry with a screwball named Jack Jonstad but he was more interested in making headlines than actually closing down some of the sleazier taverns and, like I said, we were seeing more and more customers. Yeah, we were making money but the headaches were getting larger and more painful.

That's when the Jerzies showed up and said they were here to solve all of our problems. There was a guy named Cordova Benson who looked and sounded like he came from New Jersey – and I had never been to New Jersey! The Syndicate had not invited them to show up, they just did. Walked into our board meeting with Jonstad and Eagleburger. Eagleburger was probably the most dangerous man in town. Killed a man in Wyoming or Colorado and had at least one high profile hit under his belt here in Anchorage. Or at least that was what the rumor was.

Eagleburger had made contact with the Trenton mob and told us what was going to happen. He didn't ask us if we wanted the deal, he just told us. It was not presented as if there was a choice. Three things were going to happen right away. First, all of the lounges, taverns, brothels and gambling joints between Fifth and Ship Creek were going to become members of the Anchorage Downtown Liquor Dealer's Syndicate. Second, dues were going to double and be paid by deposit to one of the banks in town – which would make them legitimate business expenses. Third, all problems from any business were to be funneled through the Syndicate. On the top of that list would be what Eagleburger called security. There would be a roving crew of *individuals* – that was the term he used – who would rove from lounge to tavern to brothel and make sure that everything was *copacetic* – and that was his term too but he pronounced the word *co-pas-tic*. These security individuals would be run by a local we knew, Harold Drochester, and he would handle all dealings with the police.

That was just about the size of it. It's not as if we, that is, the Syndicate board, talked a lot about it. It was made clear to us that this was it the way it was going to be. Half of me – and most of the board, actually – didn't like how it was presented but it was what we needed then. The less time we spent trying to break up fights, the more time we would have to sell booze. The fewer broken bottles, smashed tables and penny ante lawsuits that had to be settled out of court, the more cash we could put into the till.

There was only one thing we, collectively I mean, had a hard time understanding was why we would be paying the dues to the Syndicate as deposits to a bank. Some of the lounge owners had come from back East and knew all about protection money but it had been cash, under the table money. But here it was through bank deposits. That seemed very odd. But then again, we were all jumpy as hell because the IRS was in town in a big way.

You have to understand that when it came to the lounges, there were not that many of them when Anchorage was compared to Seattle or Portland. The bulk of us, members that is, were along about four blocks of Fourth Avenue and scattered over a dozen blocks in the downtown area and then crammed in between the cemetery and about C. The IRS didn't have to chase us all over the countryside, they would just walk down Fourth Avenue, door to door, and ask to see our books. For a few years that was exactly what they did, more to make sure that we were keeping books than looking at the numbers. They were doing it to the other industries as well, bringing us into the modern world.

So, yeah, depositing the protection money was odd. But like I said before, it was not offered to us as if we had a choice. Eagleburger was not a man you wanted to cross, Dorchester was local and had a reputation for ending physical disputes and Jonstad was one of our own. Hell, we had hired him before. So that was the way it was. We paid our dues, took the business write off and things, I hate to say this, got better.

Right away the Jerzies made sure that we had no more fights. The bouncers kept care of the drunks – we didn't have an 86 policy in those days – and when things started to get out of hand, the bouncer picked up the phone. Within a matter of minutes there was a group of men, all local, not New Jersey thugs, who showed up. We did not call them unless things got really bad because there was nothing gentle about these guys. They were ex-Marine and they didn't care who they hit. They waded into a brawl as a unit and cleaned up the situation. When they left and the police showed up, everyone was a DKN.

Then we started having problems. I can't really pinpoint when that happened but I'd say about 1958 or 1959. It had been a wild ten years and a lot had happened. The Jerzies moved in and spread out pretty quickly. They were into the lounges and taverns and then construction and some unions. What they did was needed and boy did we pay for it. But by 1958 or 1959, like I said, things began to change. The real muscle behind the Jerzies was Eagleburger and he went to Arizona. He was still calling the shots but Arizona was a long way from Anchorage. The business at that time was run by two guys from Trenton, Cordova Benson, and a behind-the- scenes guy named Al. Al something Italian. He was invisible and I, we, never really knew what the hell he was doing in Anchorage. The real power was Harold Drochester. He wasn't a Jerzie; he was local. He didn't kill people; he just beat them up. When something beyond that was needed, Eagleburger took care of it.

But by 1958 Eagleburger was gone and the protection racket was being run by Drochester and Jonstad. Drochester was doing the lifting but I don't know what the flipping burger hell Jonstad was doing. He had been the link with Eagleburger but Eagleburger was gone. Syndicate fees went straight to the bank so he wasn't doing any collecting the way it was done on the East Coast and Drochester was doing the patrolling. Jonstad basically hung out in his office in the Zabriskie-Silvestri building, in the building known as the Crystal Bath brothel and talked big.

Everyone knew that the days of the Jerzies was limited. We had needed them during the boom times but those times were gone. The war had been over by a good ten years and all of the construction projects had shut down. Those remote bases had been built so the influx of workers was over. Anchorage was a lot bigger by then, say three times what it had been after the war, but these were local folks who stayed a couple of years. It was back to the point where we didn't need the protection; our bouncers could handle the traffic.

So what did we need the Jerzies for?

The quick answer is that we didn't.

But getting out from under their hammer was not easy. The police and the feds weren't any help and Eagleburger was still muscle even though it was far away. Jonstad and Drochester were in town and checking up on the fees. We, that is, the Syndicate, talked with some lawyers to see what we could do and they said zip. The Syndicate was charging fees and that was legitimate so no laws were being broken. We could take the verbal contract to court but we could lose – *lose!* To organized crime?! Where was the *justice* in that?!

It took us about a year to come up with a strategy which was, basically, no strategy at all. Basically we would just stop paying the fees. If they didn't like it they could take us to court. Cordova Benson did a lot of threatening and we got a lot of nasty calls from Eagleburger but, frankly, by then it was all over but the shouting.

Even more important, there was going to be a new President of the United States then, John F. Kennedy, and his brother was going to be Attorney General. That Robert Kenney said right away he was going after organized crime, something that the J. Edgar Hoover had been saying for years did not exist. That put the pinch on the Jerzies because now the United States Attorney in Anchorage was taking a hard look at the Jerzies. What made it nice was that Anchorage was so small that even with a staff of three the United States Attorney could focus on the Jerzies.

But the big problem, we were told, was that the traditional way to roll up a criminal enterprise was to 'follow the money.' But in our case the money was legitimate. Fees were a normal part of business and following the money wasn't going to do diddly in Alaska. Sure, they'd look into the matter but, frankly, unless there was illegal activity there was not much they could do.

What made it worse – and we didn't know this until after we talked with the U. S. Attorney – the money that we had been paying wasn't leaving Alaska. It wasn't made clear to us why, just that it had been invested in land. In other words, the money we had paid in fees was legitimate and the money we had paid had been invested in land which made it legitimate. So no money was illegal. No illegal money meant no U. S. Attorney investigation.

Worst of all, the only thing being done that was illegal was gambling and we were the ones doing it! We were doing the illegal activity, not the Jerzies!

"Don't make a federal case out of it," the United States Attorney had said. "Contact the local police." Yeah, like that was going to work.

So we had zip. But we did have a Plan B. Plan B was to simply not pay any more protection fees. That is, we weren't going to be depositing the money into the Jerzie account any more. We kept the money in our account, the Syndicate account, until we knew what to do with it.

But we covered our bases, so to speak. We started paying Drochester and Jonstad directly because they were Alaskans. Come Hell or high water they were going to be here for a long time while Benson and his side kick were going to be gone, the sooner the better. We had an even more devious reason when we decided to pay Drochester and Jonstad. It was to drive a wedge between them and Benson and Eagleburger.

We turned out to be right for the wrong reasons. About a year later, after nothing happened, we found out that Eagleburger had dementia. He was no longer the man he once was. In fact, he couldn't even remember the man he once was. So, by 1963 it appeared that the Jerzies were on their way out. The construction money was gone, the Syndicate fees were squeezing off, the unions and the construction industries were giving them the boot and we could not figure out why they were still in town. The only thing we could think of was that Benson was keeping an eye on their real estate investment.

Then came the earthquake and here is where I've got to be careful. Your immunity deal requires that I tell the truth about everything and I will but I'm not going to speculate. I'll only tell what I know to be a fact. The instant the earthquake hit we knew we had a problem. That's right, we, the Syndicate. What had brought the Jerzies to us in the first place was the construction boom after the War. We had pretty much squeezed them out by 1964 because the construction money was gone. They had been squeezed out of the unions and the building trades and the brothels and the lounges and the taverns and every other industry they had oozed their way into in the first place.

When we backed out of paying them, everyone else did as well. That's the way it is up here. We don't talk to one another – at least not the way we did before June of 1950 – but it does not take long for the word to get around. We gave the Jerzies the boot in about 1962 and by the earthquake everyone else had followed suit. It was only a matter of moments before they left town with kit, caboodle and the kitchen sink. They were on their way out. The only thing that surprised us as to why they were still here at all after 1962.

Then, boom, along comes the earthquake. We've got buildings from the seashore to the flatlands collapsing under their own weight. The J. C. Penny's garage came tumbling down and that was a brand new structure, less than a year old. We had roads we could not drive on, an airport where no planes could land, a power plant that could not produce power, the water utility was out, a port that could not dock a barge and less than week's supply of gasoline.

It took us a day to recover our senses and get back in communication with the rest of Alaska and the West Coast. What we found out was that the damage to the quake was a heck of a lot more widespread than we had suspected. There was damage as far south as San Francisco and every coastal town in Alaska had suffered major damage. As soon as the news of the ruin reached Washington D. C. there was the announcement that there was going to be a whale of a lot of emergency disaster relief dollars. I mean, we were talking about rebuilding the whole city! The whole city! Block by block! Yes, we needed the dollars but none of us had to be told what that meant for the Jerzies. Just as we were about to get them out, back in they would come. Not a single one of us in any industry believed that the Jerzies were going to walk away from the kind of money we needed to rebuild.

Worse, with Eagleburger gone in more ways than one there was every reason to believe they would bring their own muscle from the East Coast. Kennedy had been shot and LBJ was now President. Even though Robert Kennedy was still Attorney General he was collared. He didn't have the latitude to do to organized crime what he wanted to do. So, if you were in organized crime, you had a respite. All of this was not good news for Alaska.

Everyone knew we had to move fast. I was not privy to the private meetings that went on in the other industries but I do know what happened at the board meetings of the Anchorage Downtown Liquor Dealer's Syndicate. We held one meeting with Benson, Jonstad and some guy with a broken nose from Trenton. The guy with the broken nose had come north with "Gypsy" George, the only guy who was rugged enough to fly in the days right after the earthquake. I mean, that man could land anywhere!

Anyway, these three men told us that the Trenton boys were standing by with labor and supplies to rebuild the city of Anchorage but they – Benson, Jonstad and the guy with the broken nose – were expecting things to go back the way they had been before Robert F. Kennedy became Attorney General. Eagleburger may be gone but a planeload of *assistance* – that was Cordova's term – was being packed in Trenton. This *assistance* would arrive very soon and then things could "go back to the way they were before." None of the board members said anything and the three left.

That's all that I know for a fact.

What I have heard was that hell was a poppin' all over town in the other industries. The undercurrent was the same everywhere, so palpable you could feel it. There was no way the Trenton boys were going to be allowed to get another foothold in Anchorage. But to keep them out a handful of things had to be done and done quickly. What I do know is that the Mayor of Anchorage at the time, George Sharrock, suddenly decided not to run for re-election. In his place, Elton Randolph ran for mayor. Why a banker would run for mayor was a mystery to all of us until about a year later and then we just picked up pieces of the puzzle. Yeah, you may already know but to be safe, I'll tell you what you already believe because no one told me. I just had to figure it out. The Mayor is the CEO of the city and the Chief of Police serves at the Mayor's pleasure. So if the Mayor does not want an investigation of something like, say, the demise of an individual, he just tells the Police Chief to ice box it. The case goes cold and then goes away. As long as there isn't any paperwork, it's GDBM.

Everyone knows Dorchester whacked Cordova Benson. We all knew it but there isn't a shred of proof to back that up. Who paid him, I do not know. All I do know is that the talk on the street was that Dorchester solved a problem. Jonstad, I have no clue. He just vanished into thin air. He was the Judge Crater of Alaska; he went out for dinner on evening and never came home. There was one other link to the Trenton boys and that was this low key wise guy and he could read the writing on the wall. The minute Benson, Jonstad and the guy from Trenton disappeared, he was gone. And by gone I mean he took a plane. Word has it that he flew out with "Gypsy" and never came back. Where he is I do not know. Where he is I do not want to know. All I want to know is that the Jerzies are gone and they are not coming back – ever.

That's all I have to say to you guys. I've told you everything I know for a fact and I am hiding no crime that I know of. Now turn off that damn recorder."

George "Gypsy" Davis

"The FBI wants to talk to me about after all these years? It took you bastards this long to find me and why the Hell weren't you doing your job in 1964? You leave honest people to break the law to keep their city clean and then you come back years later to dig through the charnel house for a bone or two? Jezz Louise are you guys behind the times!

Yeah, I'm "Gypsy" George. Got the name because I was a gypsy pilot. I'd fly anywhere I could to make a buck. Born in Alaska and started running mail by dog sled – and don't roll your eyes like that, FBI man! What are you, all of 22 or 23? Probably born and raised in some city with paved streets in the Lower 48, don't know squat about Alaska and here you are digging up graves from 1964. You want to know what happened then you've got to have your history right. That's the trouble with you guys with short hair and clean fingernails. You don't know your history and think that yesterday was the same as today. You want my story you've got to listen to all of it, *son.*

Like I was saying, *son,* I started out running dogs. That's important for you to keep in mind because in those days there weren't that many maps. We didn't have anything like aviation maps. We didn't even have them during the war. You had to know where you were going. The new boys had to fly with us old codgers to get the lay of the land. Getting to Fairbanks was easy, it was IFR, "I follow the Railroad," but other than that you had to know the country. I knew the country because I ran dogs all over it for 15 years. I recognized the mountains so I could find the mines and the dredges when I got the call. Were not that many pilots who knew how to find those boys. I did so I got the call. I flew where no one else could go and where no one wanted to go.

On top of that, I was one of the few who'd fly in Gillam Weather. You Outsiders don't know that that means. Back in the days after the war there were three kinds of weather. First there was "Pan American weather," when the sky was clear and the visibility unlimited. Then there was "flying weather" which ranged from good to poor, depending on who was doing the talking. Finally, there was Gillam weather, conditions that were so **bad** that only Harold "Thrill 'em, Chill 'em, Spill 'em, but no kill 'em" Gillam would fly. That's right, son, the whole name. That's what everyone called him. He picked up the name from a kid in Cordova who wrote a poem about him,

> He thrill 'em
> Chill 'em
> Spill 'em
> But no kill 'em
> Gillam.

Harold Gillam would fly in any kind of weather, and I mean *any* kind of weather. And he survived. Let me give you an idea how good he was flying in bad weather. One time in the 1940s he flew into McGrath in a storm so bad that one of the pilots on the ground said he 'wouldn't have whipped a cat out there that night.' But Gillam flew. The grounded pilots were sitting around the fireplace when they heard a plane fly in. Gillam came in, said 'Hello' to his friends, refueled his plane and took off. Three days later, those men were still in McGrath and Gillam was back in Fairbanks safe and sound.

Another time a guy from United Airlines didn't believe that Gillam had the eyes of cat so he rode with Gillam from Fairbanks to Barrow. That was a six-and-a-half-hour trip and Gillam's plane could only carry enough fuel for seven hours. The two men climbed aboard and Gillam chewed his way through several thousand feet of cloud cover and then shot north for six and half hours over an unbroken sea of clouds. Suddenly he nosed the plane down. His passenger wet his pants because all he could see was thick fog. The first objects he did see were antenna poles flashing by as Gillam landed in the Barrow lagoon. That was the kind of pilot Gillam was and that is the kind of a pilot I am and that's why they called me the Gypsy: I'd fly anywhere in any weather.

I had to. I didn't have any regular customers so I had to chase the dollars when they were available. Back in the 1950s, for example, a guy I knew in Fort Yukon – I was flying out of Fairbanks then – had a scheme to keep his hotel full during the fall. He got himself some small nuggets of gold and showed them to anyone who came through Fort Yukon and swore this gold had come from the bottom of a Native boy's fish wheel near the village. No one seemed to question that the lodge owner might have an *ulterior motive* in wanting a bunch of people to come into a town where he had the only hotel, and it did not take long for the word to leak out. In Fairbanks there was a general infection of the gold bug when he tipped the *Fairbanks Daily News Miner* and the radio station that there just might be a gold strike in Fort Yukon. All you needed was a pick, shovel, pan and a 'packsack full of grub.' That's what he said and that's what the radio announcer said and that started it all.

I figured the strike was hogwash but there were people who wanted to fly in so I took 'em. It was probably the first gold rush in world history where the stampeders were airlifted to the diggings. The strike only lasted about a week and I was making four trips a day and there were still people standing in line when the sun went down. Passengers did not pay enough so I switched to cargo, primarily beer, 3,000 pounds of it on my first flight – which was 1,000 pounds over the load limit. My plane was so overloaded I had to fly along the river because I could not make it over the mountains. I did fly some working girls out there but I was primarily flying cargo. For a week. The Great Fishwheel Gold Strike it was called. After the week I flew people back to Fairbanks. I did not instigate that strike but I sure didn't do anything to stop it.

To give you an idea of the kind of trips I would take that no one else would, just before the quake I was hired by the United States Marshal Service to pick up a man who was accused of killing his wife. When I got to Chevak I found that there was also going to be a witness coming back to Fairbanks too. My plane only had four seats and I was going to be sitting in one of them and the United States Marshal in another. That left a cold body and two warm ones. So I put the wife's corpse in one seat and the two men in the last seat. I put the witness on the husband's lap and strapped them both into a back seat with seatbelt.

Don't get all nervous, son, I'm telling you these stories so you'll understand what happened all those years ago. See, right after the war there was lots and lots of flying business. The problem was that I wasn't getting any of it. The heavy cargo came up by barge all spring, summer and fall and almost everything else came by regular airplane. I was a gypsy, get it. "Gypsy" Dave. I got the leftovers, the stuff no one else wanted to take. I wasn't a regular so I didn't get the regular passengers and I was one-man-one-plane operation so I didn't get the long term contract. I got the leavings.

But there was enough leavings for me. I flew a lot of booze into those remote military sites. As long as I landed well back from the sites I was legal. Me and a bunch of the other pilots set up a liquor distribution service getting booze out to places like Port Clarence, Romanzov, Tin City, Cape Sarichef, Sparrevohn, Attu and then to the wet and damp villages. We'd fly the booze, take our cash and leave. I, me personally, also made a lot of money on garbage runs.

Garbage runs? Son, you gotta understand the history up here to understand what went down. A garbage run was a quick-and-dirty trip in or out. It was the kind of a trip you didn't want anyone to know about. Suppose some construction worker beat up his boss. That was bad for everyone so I got called to get the guy out. The guy who beat up the supervisor, I mean. No one cared about the weather or time of year. They just wanted that guy gone and fast. So I'd land in the middle of the night take the guy aboard, sometimes in chains and sometimes passed out. My job was to get them out of wherever and to Juneau. When I got to Juneau I'd meet someone at the end of the runway, away from the terminal such as it was then, and drop this guy off with a company executive. I never asked why I was getting this guy out of the Bush and never wanted to know what happened to him later. I was part of what was known as the DKN Club, 'Don't Know Nothing,' and I liked it that way.

Now I've got to tell you another few stories to finish off with what you want to know. You clearly don't know diddly about flying so let me give you some basics. Most planes in those days flew overloaded. That was because the CAA, the Civil Aeronautics Administration, did not know what the hell they were doing. They were using Lower 48 rules in Alaska which made no sense t'all. Like, for instance, when you landed on the ice outside some of these villages, the landing strip was a cleared patch that was marked off with burning bags. You would call ahead and say you were half-an-hour out and the villagers would put some paper bags with candles inside or maybe start some small fires at the four corners of the landing area. That showed me where to land. But there were some CAA people who got their nose pulled out of joint because in the Lower 48 you cannot land where there is an open flame. So I'd get written up for landing where there was an open fire on the runway. Give me a flippin' break!

A big thing for the new-to-Alaska CAA folks was flying over-loaded. *Everyone* flew overloaded. First, because the rules for how much cargo you can take were for the Lower 48 and made no sense in Alaska. You didn't fly what the CAA called a full load to a mine and then come back for the 100 pounds you left behind. You just overloaded and as long as you didn't get crazy wild there was no problem. Another thing you non-fly boys don't understand is that planes get lighter the longer you fly them. That's right, son, they get lighter. That's because fuel is weight and the longer you fly the more fuel you use. As you burn fuel, the plane gets lighter. If you know what you are doing – and I'm still alive so that shows I knew what I was doing – you were overloaded when you took off but were not dangerously heavy when you landed.

The key to flying overloaded, and here's where you want to listen carefully, son, is to choose when to take off when you were flying cargo. All of the bush pilots knew the work schedule for the CAA yahoos and made sure that when we were going to fly overloaded we got an inspector with an IQ. There were sharp inspectors and dull knives. If I was flying light or passengers, anyone could inspect me. But if I was going to be overloaded, there were three or four inspectors over the years who let me fly as long as I wasn't doing anything that was really stupid. It's not as if they were looking the other way, they were just Alaskan in the sense they knew what was going on and doing their job with a little shaving.

Now that I've given you the background, I'll answer the question you been burning to ask: what did I do to stop the Trenton people from making it Anchorage. Well, that's a two part answer and both answers are nothing.

The first part is that right after the quake I got a garbage run from Jack Jonstad. Everyone in Anchorage knew who he was and what he did but his money was good so I took the job. No one was flying out of Anchorage because the CAA had closed the airport down. I just took off when they weren't looking. A lot of guys were doing it and there wasn't much the CAA could do about it. The only planes _not_ flying were the regularly scheduled ones. Gypsies like me flew when we wanted. My job was to fly Cordova Benson, the guy you want to know about, to Juneau to pick up some fat slob with a broken nose from Trenton, New Jersey. No, I didn't know his name then and I don't know it now. All I know is that he might as well have worn a sign that said "Organized Crime." Today you'd call him a wise guy; then I just thought of him as an @##$%^&.

I picked him up at the end of the runway in Juneau next to a warehouse. Benson called him over, he got on board and we took off. I was doing the flying and Benson was doing the talking. All the way to Anchorage. Talk about Garbanzo beans! These guys were laying out their entire strategy. I knew all about the squeezing out of the Jerzies in Anchorage – Hell, who didn't? – and what I was hearing was the Trenton plan to get back into the game.

Trenton was counting on all this emergency funding money from the Federal government to rebuild Anchorage. I'd been in Anchorage right after the quake and that meant a lot of dollars going into construction. The Jerzies were going to get a large piece of that pie. Here they were, on my airplane, talking about corruption and blackmail and washing money as if I wasn't there! All the way to Anchorage!

But this time they had even bigger plans. They were going to expand into the gaming industry big time. It was their moment to move because Alaska was going to have a new, dependable, state of the art, communication system as fast as it could be built. This meant that Alaskans could start betting on boxing, football games and horse racing in real time rather than waiting for the scores to be broadcast on a news program.

Even more important, the Jerzies had worked out the two wrinkles of squeezing money from Alaskans. The two problems were allowing bets to be placed from the remote military and support bases across Alaska and paying the winners. The Jerzies were tired of dealing with Anchorage bankers and tired of seeing their skim go into land which may or may not pay off over the long run. They wanted their skim in cash immediately. Instead of using Alaskan banks they were going to use Trenton banks. The betting would be handled out of Anchorage but the actual money would be paid into accounts in Trenton banks. Then the winner would withdraw money by writing checks from the Trenton bank account. This would make the winner on the remote bases happy because they could verify their winnings by phone. It made the Jerzies happy because the bets would be placed in Trenton, a long way from the slippery hands of the Anchorage bankers. The Jerzies were doubly happy because the total population of the remote military bases, support facility and Bush residents who could use the White Alice system was more than 20,000. That made them the largest 'city,' so to speak, in the state. Even more important, 100% of them were working and had the money to gamble.

The only problem was using the military communication system from the remote locations to Anchorage to place bets. They planned on avoiding complications by establishing a private phone on each of the bases and hiring someone to manage the buying and selling on-site. This was somewhat legal since a lot of people were pretty much doing the same thing. Servicemen and military employees were already buying shirts, shoes, toothpaste, radios and firearms over the military network so making bets was not a stretch.

All the Jerzies had to do to start a bookie operation was to come north with a few electronic devices, each the size of suitcase. They could use the emergency military communication system that was going up to connect Alaska to the lower states and then the commercial lines when they were back in service. Courtesy of the federal reconstruction money and the remote gambling income, the Jerzies expected to be in Alaska *forever.*

Well, I get back to Anchorage and the first thing I was told was that I was to fly back to Juneau the next day and pick up a dozen people from Trenton. That was going to be two trips because my plane was a six-passenger job. The guys from Trenton had come in to Juneau by regular airlines but had to fly to Anchorage on a gypsy because the Anchorage airport was still officially down. I knew what these guys were going to do when they got to Anchorage. How the hell could I not know? I'd just spent four hours listening to the plans!

What did I do?

What did I do?!

I flew to Juneau to pick up the wise guys! That was what I had been paid to do! So I flew to Juneau. And you know, sometimes *strange* happened between the time I left Anchorage and the time I reached Juneau. Somehow the United States military found out that the Trenton wise guys were going to be using the military communication system for gambling purposes. Someone in the military in Anchorage called the Pentagon who called the United States Attorney in New Jersey who issued search warrants for gambling devices in the possession of individuals who may – or may not – have crossed a state line with such devices to be used on the United States military communication system for the purposes of gambling. The search warrants were wired to Juneau on the civilian system so the Juneau rumor mill had the story before the United States Marshal got to the airport.

Apparently the government wanted to talk with them and they were ordered held in Juneau for questioning. A couple of them had guns which raised *another* issue – you know, entering the United States with a concealed weapon – and then some gambling paraphernalia showed up. Playing cards, I think. Apparently smuggled them into a territory of the United States as well.

So, when I landed in Juneau and rolled to the end of the runway where I had picked up the wise guy two days earlier, there was no one there. I went into Juneau and put in a call to Benson but he was gone – and in his case, *gone* was a permanent verb. Then I called Jonstad and he was gone too, another permanent verb. I finally reached Drochester who said that the Trenton passengers had been delayed and I was to wait in Juneau.

So I did.

At the best hotel in town, the Baranof.

With the tab going to the Anchorage Downtown Liquor Dealer's Syndicate.

For five days.

Then I was contacted by Drochester to come back to Anchorage that plans had changed.

That's about all I can remember.

Just a second, **son**, before you shut that recorder thing down, I've got a bit of bush pilot wisdom for you to take away from this conversation. It will give you something to chew on as you fly back to your cushy office in D. C. There are three things that are absolutely useless to a pilot: the air above you, the runway behind you and what happened a tenth of a second ago. Cordova Benson is gone, Jack Jonstad is gone and the only person in Anchorage from New Jersey now is called a tourist. All you are going to be able to do about all the nonsense that happened during the Alaska Earthquake is write a history book because that's all that's left, the runway behind you."

Samuel Smith

"One of my favorite quotes is from Alaskan humorist Warren Sitka: Life would be perfect if it weren't for sentences that start with the words *but* or *however.* That's been the story of my life. As an auditor, I mean. I'm one of those dull little men called a *bureaucrat* who gets real excited when the numbers in the columns at the bottom of a sheet add up and match. That's me, the bureaucrat.

While I am personally as dull as dishwater – I'm an *accountant* for heavens's sake – I have a statement I stole from someone that I like to use every once in a while. I say that I am involved with the *drama of origination.* I am the person who sees the first proof of success. At the same time, I see the first blossoms of fraud and corruption as well. I know what I see but I cannot do anything about it; that takes place above my head. I just send my concern up the chain of command.

I came to Alaska at the start of the war and was one of about 50 men assigned to keep track of the Lend-Lease equipment and supplies at Ladd Field outside of Fairbanks. I came from Duluth so the weather didn't bother me but the Russians sure did. Accounting to them wasn't even a black art; they didn't even do it. They'd load up their planes – our planes, actually – they'd load up their planes with every spare anything they could find in Fairbanks to take to Russia. I mean things like forks, knives, spoons, plates, pans, stuff you'd think they already had. But then again, it was free here so they took it. Jammed their planes full and took off leaving me to try to balance the books. Didn't work so I didn't. The United States government didn't either. Once the big boys knew what was happening they just said to do the best we could and left it at that. So we did and somewhere in Washington D. C. is a long list of equipment and supplies that went missing between 1941 and 1945 courtesy of the Russians.

By the time the war had ended I was married to an Anchorage girl and we came here to live. I got a job at a bank and kept books for the next ten years. Like I said before, I'm not the most inspiring individual so I didn't have any problem fitting in with the rest of the banking community. Just about everyone in the banking industry is dull, just like me.

Myrna and I raised two kids, a boy and girl. He's a graduate of Gonzaga and works in Chicago for a stock broker and my daughter married a Lt. who's now a Colonel and they are stationed in the Philippines. I retired from the banking business in 1962 and stayed home. Myrna worked for the Methodist Church part time and I was volunteering for the Unitarian Service Committee – we're a two-faith family.

I got back into the accounting business in 1962, right after I retired from the bank. I had wanted to spend my time at home growing flowers during the summer and dreaming of Hawaii during the winter but I got a call – an odd call, from an old friend from my Army days. By an odd call, I mean just that. We were both in our 60s – he looked it but I didn't – and he had gone on up the chain of command and was working at the Pentagon. They, the Army that is, were trying to close the books on the war when they came across a strange account in Anchorage. There was some Lt. Col. who had personally signed out hundreds of thousands of dollars of equipment that was never returned. But it was not high value equipment like planes or bulldozers. It was supplies like sleeping bags and radios, medical supplies, some guns, Jeeps, flame throwers, boots by the hundreds. Stuff like that. It wasn't that much of a big deal because most of that kind of stuff was being sold by the ton and ending up in military surplus stores around the world. The problem was that it was all personally authorized by a guy by the name of Dwight David Eisenhower who had been President of the United States and no one wanted to pester the old man. But you know accountants; the matter had to be closed. The only reasonable way to close the books was to find the Lt. Col. who had signed for the supplies. The man's name was Robert H. Johnson, III and he was listed in the Anchorage phone book. Did I know him?

Yeah, I said. He's my neighbor. Want me to ask him about the supplies?

Yup, said my friend, and that was the start of my friendship with Robert H. Johnson, III. He was a Mormon but that didn't, doesn't bother me. I know he doesn't wear the magic underwear because we go camping together but I've never seen him have so much as sip a beer. I can't tell you what he told me but that's not why I'm telling you about Robert.

Two years later, when the earthquake hit, Anchorage was completely cut off from the rest of the world for about a week. You could fly in and out of the city but when it came to doing business it took a while to catch up. One of the things that was desperately needed in those early days was a federal accountant to keep track of the disaster funds that were going to be coming in.

Everyone knew the money was going to be coming but the cash was needed right away. I mean the city was a shambles. There was massive damage from what is now Earthquake Park to the Ship Creek and from the Inlet to the flatlands. Everything had to be rebuilt but the immediate problem was making homes livable. Immediately. There were people, quite literally, living on the street.

Since I had experience dealing with the federal government as an accountant, the new Mayor, whom I knew personally, asked me to help. What could I do, I was only an accountant? Well, he said, you know people in Washington D. C. See if you can get approval for the banks to get loans out to people to rebuild. We know the money's coming; find us a way to get money out to the people who need it as fast as possible.

So I talked to Robert who made some calls and one of them was to an old friend of his in the Pentagon. He put me in touch with that friend who worked in the Office of Emergency Management or whatever it was called then. That was the office that gave out the money in those days. He and I talked for about an hour and we came up with a procedure for giving out the money and that was that. You can't do that today; in 1964 that was how the money was dispensed. Today you've got to have all kinds of paperwork. In 1964 you just had to have a signature and a lot of times it was your own.

So there I was, handing out hundreds of thousands of dollars on my own say so. Of course, I didn't just hand money out to anyone. A lot of folks I knew personally and some from the bank. Those folks I knew to be honest were not a problem and if I didn't know them and a local banker vouched for them that was good enough for me.

But that was the uptown crowd.

It was the downtown crowd where disaster struck.

See, when it came to the uptown people, they were all living in homes on land that was tied to the homes. When they sold the home, the land went with the sale. Downtown was a different kettle of fish. The person who owned the land might not own the building on top of it. Or the lot might have been parceled out to many different structures that were owned by a conglomerate of people. Or no one. There was property owned by people who did not exist, people who had died, *dbas*, people who were phony businesses, the whole lot. Along the whole of what we called the lounge strip, Fourth Avenue from about F Street to C Street, there were fewer than a handful of pieces of property where the building and property beneath it were owned by the same person and you could reach out and touch that person.

The only bit of good news was that the entire lounge strip – that's where I had the most problem – was going to be razed. That meant I didn't have to worry about emergency money to rebuild the structures. That was welcome news because I did not have the slightest idea how I was going to dole out money to people who did not exist, had died or who had title problems.

My problem was figuring out who to pay for the damaged buildings that were not going to be repaired. When I started to write checks for people who were outside of Alaska I ran smack dab into the Department of Justice. The Attorney General at that time was Robert F. Kennedy. His brother had been killed the previous year but he was still the Attorney general and he hated organized crime. That didn't meant much to me at the time because I thought that organized crime was something that happened on the East Coast. But when I got into the land records along the lounge strip I saw exactly what had been happening. So when I came across a land owner from New Jersey, I simply gave the money to the Department of Justice. If the New Jersey people wanted their money they could get it from the Department of Justice.

That took care of the money but not the land title. So I invented a system to handle that problem. Remember I said that I loved the *drama of origination*? Well, I had to do something and I had to do it fast. There was too much damage to move slow and too much danger in moving fast. So I created an umbrella company, so to speak, which received all of the land titles and building ownership on both sides of Fourth Avenue from F Street to C Street for all building that could not be repaired or for whom the land or building ownership was questionable. I created a board of directors and then had the federal government buy the strip. That way the money would be immediately available to the legitimate owners. The questionable owners could work out an arrangement with the umbrella company. As far as I know everything worked out well for the Alaskans. That was my only priority. I don't have any idea what happened to the money for the land and property owned by those men from New Jersey."

Jon Anderson

"1964? You have got to be kidding! It took you guys that long to figure out that something went wrong? Been *s-l-e-e-p-i-n-g* on the job?! Now don't give me this song and a dance that 'it just came to your attention' or you've 'been **busy**!' That was one of the worst kept secrets in Anchorage and everyone with badge – local, state and federal – knew exactly what went down and you federal boys didn't give a hairy rat's potato then. So why now?

Yeah, I remember Cordova Benson or whatever his name really was. He and two other guys vanished during the Earthquake. We kinda, sorta found Benson but I don't think anyone really knows what happened to the others. Word was that they had been in the J. C. Penny's garage when it went down and they were just two of the deaths associated with the quake. Benson was under a pile of bricks and cement at the old Empress Theater and the only reason he wasn't considered an earthquake death because he supposedly had two holes in his head. I'm the one who saw the holes and what happened next made me a pluralist – and you can look that up in your Funk & Wagnalls.

I started working for the Anchorage Police Department during the Korean War. Had just finished boot when the war broke out and I was sent to Korea. What a cluster that was!

United Nations troops that were basically American troops and we got the living bejeezus beat out of us. I didn't even get a chance to move forward before we were advancing to the rear. We outnumbered the North Koreans almost two to one and here we were retreating.

I was in the last group to cross the Naktong River onto the Pusan Peninsula and we took the brunt of pounding for the next month and a half, August 4th to September 18th. Every day we had incoming: mortars, rockets, bullets, bombs, you name it we took it. The river was pretty wide but it was so shallow a man could wade across and those North Koreans did. In spades. First time they came across we were taken by surprise and had to retreat. Then we came back strong and drove them back. It was not fun times, let me tell you. I was one of those guys that came back to statewide with an embroidered jacket that read **When I die I'm going to heaven because I spent the war in Korea.**

I had grown up in Bremerton, Washington and there was no way I was going back there after the Korean War. It was a city of about 25,000 then – and not a helluva lot bigger now – and there wasn't a job to be had. I mean, that's why I had joined the military, to get the hell out of town. My dad had been a security guard and the one connection he had was with a local policeman by the name of Hank Miller. Miller had left Bremerton a couple of years earlier and ended up in Anchorage as the Chief of Police. Now there was a professional! He was turning a small town police force into a professional organization. He was a martinet but the Anchorage police needed it; there were just too many loose cannons. When you worked for Hank Miller you were trained and were expected to do everything by the book. That's what eventually got him dumped but that's another story.

So, in 1952 I showed up in Anchorage with an employment letter from Hank Miller. The first thing he told me on the first day of the job was that in Anchorage you do everything by the book and that was that. No 'good to see you, son,' or 'how's your old man?' That was how Hank operated. Everyone called him 'Hank' except to his face. Then he was 'Chief.'

I was told that Anchorage had calmed down a bit in the past few years but, you know, I didn't see it that way. It was wild. But then again, I came from a small town that never got big. Looking back on it I have to say that things were pretty organized by 1953. There was an understanding, I guess that's the term for it, between the military and the city and feds and the Anchorage Downtown Retail Liquor Dealer's Syndicate as to who was responsible for what. The military had its police on the street and they took care of the shave tails and noncom. We handled the Ps, PFCs and Airmen. That's how the base wanted it handled; rank has its privileges. But we only handled problems from the lounge doorway to the street. What happened inside the lounges was handled by the liquor dealers. They had their own muscle and didn't want us in the way. That was fine with us, the police that is, because we didn't want to go into the dark lounges and break up fights. There was more than enough to do for the dozen cops on payroll.

Don't be me wrong. We did go into the lounges and brothels quite a bit. We just didn't go in to stop fights. We went in when there was a problem, usually involving some muckety muck who had to be escorted to a cab or north of Sixth Avenue. They were the kind of guys whose name was in paper a lot and we couldn't arrest them and we couldn't ignore them so we just relocated them. But they'd come back and we knew 'em by name and they knew us by name and when we showed up they just kind of packed it in.

The guy who was really the show on the lounge strip was a guy named Eagleburger. We were all told he had killed a man in Wyoming and spent ten years in jail. There was also a rumor swirling that he had taken out a cop but if he had no one I knew could come up with a name. It might have been what you now call an urban myth, something that might have happened but no one can point to a specific person. But he was a very bad dude. No less a person that Hank Miller told me that on one of my first days on patrol. He said that Eagleburger was a very dangerous man, that he was unpredictable and be very wary around him or any of his associates. I was not told to handle him with kid gloves or give him any kind of special consideration. That was the way Hank was; everyone got the same treatment. But then again, I was to watch Eagleburger like a hawk because he was one dangerous fellow.

It took me about a year to put the pieces together. I'd come from a small town so I had experience at figuring out things no one was talking about. The Anchorage Downtown Retail Liquor Dealer's Syndicate was just the front for a bunch of guys including Eagleburger, Cordova Benson and Jack Jonstad. Benson was out of New Jersey and you didn't have to be from New Jersey to know that. He might as well as had a jacket that read 'wise guy' on the back. But he wasn't a violent guy; that was Eagleburger's job. At least that's the way I read it.

Jonstad was the bag man. And a very unlikely bag man. He was all of about five feet tall and built like a tent pole. At one time he had had red hair but by the time I knew him he was bald. A pasty bald at that and he had skin rashes all over his face. He always wore long sleeves which, at that time, meant he had skin rashes all over his body. Twenty years later people who always wore long sleeves were drug addicts hiding needle marks.

Like I said, Jonstad was the bag man and an odd one at that. He didn't collect money. I mean, that's what bag men usually do. But in Anchorage no one was collecting money. Money as in cash. All of the money was being deposited in the banks. There were three or four banks at that time, depending on what you mean by a *bank*. Money from the collecting was deposited in the banks, which I was told but do not know for a fact, was because then it would be called a business expense. *Business expense!* That was rich! Protection money being written off as a business expense! I'll bet the IRS loved that!

So Jonstad wasn't really doing anything. He was just hanging out at the Crystal Bathhouse, getting laid because with a skin condition like his he had to pay for it, and generally doing nothing but checking with the banks every now and again to make sure that money was being deposited. Benson was doing, hell, I don't know what he was doing. He was always around, showing a presence but I never saw him do anything. I never heard that he did anything either. He was just kind of there, like a bar fly. There was another guy from New Jersey but I rarely saw him. I guess he had the good sense to keep his head down. I saw him from time to time until the quake and then he disappeared. Seemed to be a lot of that then. Before the quake there was handful of wise guys and after, poof, they were gone.

I guess you could say I was lucky to be Anchorage in those years. I saw the end of the frontier and the beginning of the modern age. The city was bursting at its seams with construction dollars when I first started and by the time I retired we had internet connection with the Lower 48, the library had an electronic card catalog, there was a McDonald's and the most popular bar in town had live monkeys behind Plexiglas the length of the counter. I was on the streets of Anchorage during that transition.

But you want to know about Cordova Benson. OK, here's the background. When I got to Anchorage the muscle on the lounge strip was Eagleburger. He was the very bad boy with very bad friends who broke up fights in the lounges. I had been told to keep my distance from him and I did. When I finally met him about a year after I got to Anchorage, say, 1954 or 1955, he was a shell of what he once been. He was obese, had diabetes and couldn't remember his name. This was the guy who ran

Anchorage? He couldn't tie his shoes without help and I was supposed to worry about him?

His friends? What friends? I never saw any bar brawls so he didn't need any muscle. The Anchorage economy was on a downswing, dropping from boom to bust. By 1956 the construction dollars had dried up. The military money was still there because of what are now Elmendorf and Fort Richardson and that was steady money. But the construction money was gone. Then, quite predictably, as soon as the lounge strip didn't need the muscle, everyone stopped paying for it. When the construction businesses could get enough local workers they stopped importing it. Eagleburger left for Arizona about then and the muscle business dried up.

But the Jerzies didn't leave. I don't know for a fact but my guess is that they had to stay because they had been sinking mob money into land. That's where the money was in those days: you'd buy raw land as close to downtown as you could get it because that's where the buildings were going to be built. Anything south of the airfield – the Park Strip today – was solid gold. Since the money was there and the banks were there and the land was there, everyone including the Jerzies were dropping money into land. The banks liked it because in those days they were family operations. By that I mean that the families owned the banks so they held the title to the property. They could not lose. If and when the property was paid off, the bank profited. If the property went into foreclosure, the bank simply took the title.

The impact was a land buying boom and a lot of people became what I call dishonest, honest people. These are people who know that what they are doing was a bad idea, even dishonest, but because the money was there and they could make a pile of it quickly they adjusted their morals to make the money. They don't look at themselves as *bad* people, just people taking advantage of a business opportunity. It's never a good idea to get involved with organized crime but these banking families didn't care. That was where the money was so they went for it. The bad part is that over the long run they made out like the bandits they were which is a very sorry commentary on America.

Yeah, I know this a long way around to answering your question but this background is important.

The big change came in 1960 when John F. Kennedy became President of the United States and his brother, Robert F., went after organized crime. Organized crime across the country had gotten a pass before that. Suddenly every United States Attorney in America was going after organized crime figures and associations. There must have been a lot of pressure on the Trenton mob because they started selling land. I'm guessing that was to pay legal fees. If the feds can't get you behind bars they will drive you into bankruptcy. Works either way for me.

I really don't know when the land selling started but I do know that the mob was selling land in a big way by 1962. I know that because that's when there were real uptown problems. Now the financial pressure was on the bankers. There were threats by long distance phone calls, some buildings getting burned, that kind of stuff. There was nothing you could put your finger on and say for certain it was done by the Jerzies but the message was clear.

But the bankers didn't care. They didn't have to. They had been making a killing by selling land to the Jerzies. The Jerzies had been buying the land and paying for it with dues – and I use that term loosely – from their enterprises. But by 1960 those dues had dried up or were drying up so the land started to go into default. The Jerzies didn't have the muscle to scare the bankers so they had to start selling. So the bankers started closing out the loans for cash at a steep discount. That created a firestorm because the Jerzies knew they were being cheated but couldn't do a thing about it. They didn't have local muscle anymore, the feds were watching every move they made in New Jersey and they were losing money in Alaska on land deals, in

New Jersey to lawyers and their income stream in both Alaska and New Jersey was being pinched off with federal indictments.

Here's where we get to what you want to know. Up until the earthquake the Jerzies were in a death spiral. They had no money coming in, were being forced to sell land for 10 or 15 cents on the dollar and didn't have the local muscle to change the situation. That all changed with the Alaska Earthquake.

Within a matter of days.

The instant the Jerzies read of the Earthquake they got dollar signs in their eyes. For all intents and purposes the entire city of Anchorage had to be rebuilt. All of it. That meant another construction boom. They saw the rebuilding as a chance to reboot their empire in Anchorage. But this time they were going to do what they had not done before; bring in their own muscle. The plan was to not only rebuild the city but to take over all of the lounges, brothels and gambling enterprises. Who was going to stop them? There were only about 20 cops in the city and the United States Attorney had a staff of maybe five people. It was the Wild West again.

Buildings were still coming down when one of the heavies from Trenton arrived in Anchorage. He took a tour of the city and began planning the takeover. He made a call and a dozen wise guys from New Jersey got on a plane in Trenton and made it as far as Juneau before things began to go wrong.

The big difference between Anchorage and everywhere else in America is that we are an isolated community. We are so far from everywhere else that we have to depend on each other to survive. People who hate each other's guts will work together for the common good because we have no choice. We knew that a Jerzie heavy was coming to town before he landed. We knew what he was planning to do before he made his phone call. Somehow the muscle from Trenton never made it to Anchorage. I was told they got waylaid in Juneau and were sent back East.

But that was only half the problem. The other problem was that we had three people in Anchorage who had to be removed from the scene. As long as they stayed in town there was every reason to expect the Jerzies to be back. There was Cordova Benson, Jack Jonstad and the new guy from Trenton whose name escapes me. Within a matter of days after the quake Jack Jonstad and the guy from New Jersey vanished. It was like Black Magic. Poof, they were gone. Jonstad left his office one day and never returned. So did the Jerzie muscle man. He was gone too. Neither of them got on a plane headed anywhere. They just vanished. There was another Jerzie guy in town, a very low key player, and he flew out.

Cordova Benson was another matter altogether. He did show up again.

But he was dead.

Right after the earth stopped shaking we – the police and fire, that is – were on 18 hour shifts. There were problems everywhere. Anchorage was a war zone and I've been in a war zone so I know what I am talking about. We were kicking out stuck doors in apartment buildings, looking for people buried under rubble, stopping looting – stuff like that. I was sent out to investigate the report of a person trapped under a collapsed brick wall of the old Empress Theater on Third Avenue. Two of us went out to the site, about where Barrow and Third are today, and started digging through the rubble. That's where we found Benson. He'd been shot twice in the back of his head and buried under the rubble.

That was the start of my journey to become a pluralist. Just in case you don't know what that means, a pluralist is someone who can hold two or more completely different value systems at the same time. It's like believing in what the Democrats say and what the Republicans say at the same time. Before finding Benson I had this moral code which told me what was right and what was wrong and I didn't do the wrong things. As a cop I found that code to be somewhat adjustable because sometimes it was better to look the other way than cause a problem. A lot of people make mistakes and you can ruin someone's life by pushing a point. A lot of times I didn't. I just let it pass.

But with Benson there wasn't room for a pass. He had been murdered. I didn't need a coroner to tell me that. I couldn't miss it. Me and my partner – he's dead now – could not tape off the crime scene because we didn't have any tape. Even if we had had tape we would not have used it. We were more interested in finding the living than investigating the dead so we took the body to the makeshift morgue and went back out on the street. We listed the discovery of the body in the daily log book the way we were supposed to and then left the station. Benson wasn't going anywhere and there were still living people to save. We had every intention to fill out the official paperwork later.

Six hours later my partner and I got called to the morgue and there, on the cement floor, was a manikin where we had dumped Benson's body.

Yeah, that's right. A manikin, the kind of a mock human that you dress up in a clothing store window. A manikin. The sergeant started giving me and my partner hell for reporting that this manikin, this wooden rendition of a human being lying on the floor, had been what we found under the brick rubble of what was left of the Empress Theater. When we said that 'no, we had found the body of Cordova Benson and we knew Benson by sight and we also knew that he had been shot and killed,' the sergeant went into this long tirade about what idiots we were to have mistaken a manikin for a body and we were damn lucky Anchorage was in the middle of an earthquake otherwise we'd have been fired on the spot for a stupid mistake like this one. We were ordered back out onto the street and that was the last time anyone in authority asked about Cordova Benson until you guys showed up."

Special Treasury Agent Jones

S pecial Treasury Agent Jones was faceless because he did not exist. Or, rather, he existed only on paper and only as a place holder. Or, rather, a name holder. His – or hers – was a name in the churning sea of paperwork that indicated a specific individual who would remain faceless and nameless even as his/her work was the foundation for the investigation to follow. He – or she – was not an undercover agent in the sense that he or she was inserted into an illegal activity to provide an inside look. Again, he – or she – did not exist. Maybe.

He or she might have even been a combination of people. Or not. No one knew. No one cared. That was not the point. The point was that a complete story could only be told through documents that were collected by one, two or many faceless, nameless individuals generically called researchers. They went where they went, examined what they examined, culled haystacks for needles and searched salt shakers for sugar crystals. Needle by crystal by receipt by land title he/she/they pieced together stories that were never supposed to see the light of day.

In the real world, the one in which Jones did **not** live, there are two genres of documents: public and private. A public document is one which is filed in public offices and can be seen by members of the public. A private document, conversely, is one that is not accessible to the public. A good example of a transaction that involves both is the selling of a plot of land. The Division of Lands does not care how much a plot of land was purchased for or, for that matter, how much the land is worth. The Division only wants to know who owns the property. This information is available to the public, often on-line. The ownership of the land, be the owner an individual, trust, bank or corporation, is a public document. The contract between buyer and seller is a private document. A member of the public cannot legally see that contract without the permission of the buyer or the seller.

In the world of Special Treasury Agent Jones no such distinction of documents existed. No document was safe from the scrutiny of Jones. If it was on-line he can find it. If it was in an archive, she could retrieve it. If it was in a law suit the courts would release it. If it was in a bottom drawer of a desk, a search warrant would reveal it. The information could have been uncovered by the IRS, part of a routine audit, a proprietary conflict of interest filing or part of an ATF search and seizure. It could have been a Social Security questionnaire or from an FBI docket. It could have been provided by someone who did not know what it was or someone who did and was adverse to a prison sentence. It could have arrived in an unmarked envelope or been handed in by a whistleblower. The Jones of the world do not know from whence the documents come, only that they exist and by the simple fact they have arrived means that there is a provenance. His/her/their concern was not how the document(s) arrive but the truth they contain.

But there was one aspect of the documentation that Special Treasury Agent Jones could not control and that was the temporality. The documents were gathered when they were gathered but this did not mean said documents arrived in chronological sequence. The documents could be a decade old. That was fine with Jones because what mattered was the story the documents told, not the sequence in which the paperwork was collected. This, however, was the great flaw in the churning wheels of justice. The unfortunate fact of the matter is that sometimes the wheels of justice turn too slowly and then vengeance is left to the Lord Who, it would appear, is capricious in the application of punishment.

This, however, was not the concern of Jones. What was the concern of Jones was the possibility that somewhere somehow someone might be evading punishment for an act committed yesterday, last week or a decade earlier.

It was not until well into the 1970s that the multi-faceted case against a New Jersey crime family was put to bed. By the time the sentences were read, only six of the original 29 defendants were present in court. The rest were deceased, in witness protection programs or too demented to know their first names let alone the charges they faced. The six present in court plead guilty to attempting to start and run a criminal operation in Alaska using an exclusive United States government communications system. The six were found guilty and sentenced to a year in prison which they had already served before they had been released on bail. They had other charges to face in other courts, state and federal, and at the time of their sentencing all were in hock into the millions to their lawyers.

The lawyers for this particular case had been paid in land titles. The land had been legally purchased in the boom days of Anchorage and, at the time, had been touted as prime real estate as the city of Anchorage was expected to move in that direction. It was true that the city was moving in that direction. But it was also true that land has a fluid title. It may belong to the land owner on paper but can be superseded by residency. That is indeed what was discovered by the lawyers for the New Jersey defendants. It was not until the Arab Oil Embargo sent the market price of petroleum up and provided the catalyst for the Trans-Alaska Oil Pipeline that the lawyers spent the money for a plane ticket to assess their acquired holdings in Anchorage. It was only then they discovered that the land had passed through a series of owners beginning with squatters and thereafter mall developers.

When the lawyers tried to unravel the provenance, they were told that the owners of record had been John "Jack" Jonstad and Geraldo Sandro Andretti, neither of whom had answered any of the numerous letters and notices sent to their addresses. After a number of years a default judgment had been filed and the land went to the bank. The bank had been paying the municipal taxes during which time various families had squatted on the property and thus, under Alaskan law, the squatters were entitled to claim it as their own.

This they had done legally.

In 1971, seven years after the Alaska Earthquake.

A protest by the lawyers lead to an investigation which was presented to them by the Department of Justice. It was a compendium of the investigation of Special Treasury Agent Jones who stated that all legal aspects of all land in question had been examined and the land had been legally acquired by the squatting families who had then sold the real estate to a land development conglomerate which had created a handful of malls on the acreages. As no crime had been committed the United States Department of Justice and the State of Alaska Attorney General's Office had no grounds for further investigation.

There was, however, a single plot that had evaded the squatters' monument marks and for which property taxes had been and were still being paid. It was approximately half an acre in size, swampy and immediately adjacent to an abandoned pioneer sewage lagoon, the reason it had not been settled by the squatters or converted into a mall. The Municipal Land office stated that since the taxes had been paid, the land could be turned over to the lawyers for a modest transfer fee. Upon personal examination of the acreage it was found to be chocked with Devil's Club, a fitting tribute to the Biblical prophecy that what goes around does indeed come around – sometimes it just takes a while to get there.

www.ingramcontent.com/pod-product-compliance
Lightning Source LLC
Chambersburg PA
CBHW052042090426
42739CB00010B/2022